for Heidi, Nina and Felix

About Me &

I'm a food-loving mum and former early years teacher living in Norfolk with my husband, three children (Heidi, 6, Nina, 4 and Felix, 1) and our pet cat, Bella. When my eldest daughter started on solids in 2016, I started the Baby Led Kitchen Instagram account to have a bit of fun sharing my recipes and tips. It grew and grew, and as followers kept asking for more recipes, I decided to leave my teaching job and create the Baby Led Kitchen app, so more people could have the recipes at their fingertips. To date the app has 230 recipes and tens of thousands of downloads from across the world.

All of my recipes and tips have busy family lives in mind. Our house is frequently chaotic, but also full of laughter and creativity. We love to cook, sing, dance and spend time together outdoors. I spend most of my days checking my phone too often, conjuring up new recipes, changing nappies, playing Paw Patrol and asking people to put their shoes on. I wrote most of this book on broken sleep, whilst my youngest napped and when the children were in bed – and I am immensely proud of the result. I hope you enjoy our family recipes as much as we do and that reading this helps you feel confident to support your baby on their own weaning journey.

Intuitive Weaning

For calm mealtimes and happy babies

Jo Weston

Founder of Baby Led Kitchen

Vermilion
LONDON

Intuitive Weaning

*For calm
mealtimes
and happy
babies*

Jo Weston

Founder of Baby Led Kitchen

Vermilion
LONDON

for Heidi, Nina and Felix

About Me &

I'm a food-loving mum and former early years teacher living in Norfolk with my husband, three children (Heidi, 6, Nina, 4 and Felix, 1) and our pet cat, Bella. When my eldest daughter started on solids in 2016, I started the Baby Led Kitchen Instagram account to have a bit of fun sharing my recipes and tips. It grew and grew, and as followers kept asking for more recipes, I decided to leave my teaching job and create the Baby Led Kitchen app, so more people could have the recipes at their fingertips. To date the app has 230 recipes and tens of thousands of downloads from across the world.

All of my recipes and tips have busy family lives in mind. Our house is frequently chaotic, but also full of laughter and creativity. We love to cook, sing, dance and spend time together outdoors. I spend most of my days checking my phone too often, conjuring up new recipes, changing nappies, playing Paw Patrol and asking people to put their shoes on. I wrote most of this book on broken sleep, whilst my youngest napped and when the children were in bed – and I am immensely proud of the result. I hope you enjoy our family recipes as much as we do and that reading this helps you feel confident to support your baby on their own weaning journey.

contents

~~~

If we understand our baby's development and eating behaviours, we can more easily listen to them and trust in their instincts

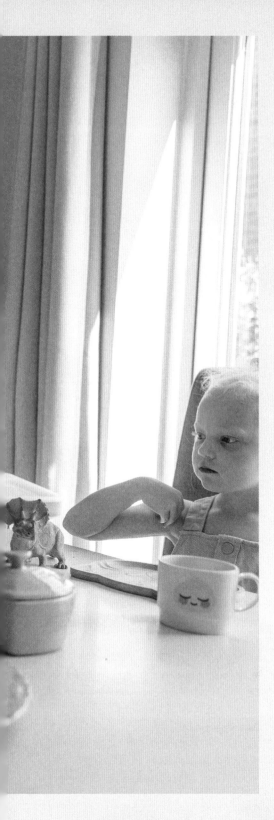

Introduction

Starting solids is a big milestone in your baby's life. To date, milk has provided comfort, connection and energy for your baby. Now, the introduction of food brings social interaction, joy, celebration and memories. Watching your baby experience their first tastes of food can be exhilarating. They are opening a door to a world they never knew existed.

Exciting as this may be, weaning can be stressful. Parents put pressure on themselves to get it right and frequently worry that they are doing it wrong. Conflicting advice from social media, literature and well-meaning family members can cause great confusion, too. I want to reassure you that adding food to your baby's diet is easier than you might think. *Intuitive Weaning* will help you to calmly support your baby as they follow their feeding instincts.

I have written this book as a mum of three, a teacher and the creator of the Baby Led Kitchen recipe app and Instagram account. I speak daily with parents from all around the world about weaning. This has given me a deep understanding of the common challenges and worries that parents encounter at different stages of their baby's introduction to food. In this book I answer the questions that I am asked the most, and explore important areas that are seldom visited in weaning books. While most available literature focuses predominantly on early nutrition, *Intuitive Weaning* is largely written from a child development perspective. My professional background is in early education, not in dietetics. However, I always lean on professional advice and research, which I have reflected in this book as much as possible.

This book is not about teaching your baby to eat or telling you exactly what to feed them – far from it. *Intuitive Weaning* will first help you to understand the important basics of weaning that you need to know, then take a much deeper look into *how* your baby might respond to starting solids – and *why*. My theory is that if we understand our baby's development and eating behaviours, we can more easily listen to them and trust in their instincts. This will help them to build a positive connection to food and to reap the benefits of colourful, tactile mealtimes. The book also tackles practical, everyday challenges that are often missing from weaning books. In the second half of this book, you will find a wealth of baby-friendly family

It is very easy for parents to fall into the trap of placing 'rule' above 'baby'

recipes, all of which I have created and cooked myself.

My inspiration for writing this book comes partly from my own struggles with eating as a teenager and young adult. We know that a child's early eating experience can shape their relationship with food as an adult. It concerns me that many parents feel under pressure to 'wean' their children in certain ways and with certain 'rules'. I receive messages from parents who are feeling anxious about their children's diets before they have even eaten a single floret of broccoli or a mouthful of carrot mash! I believe that we need to do everything in our power to make sure that our babies' early experiences with food are positive and relaxed, in order to help them to develop a healthy relationship with food from day one.

We must not let any personal hang

ups around food or our bodies trickle into another generation. We need to focus on keeping the dinner table calm and accepting – free from too many adult-imposed rules around food. Why not start from day one of weaning? Remember that you are the most important role model for your baby – it's really important that they see you eating and enjoying food. The recipes in this book are developed so that the whole family can enjoy them together, when possible. I have considered *you* in my recipe development, not just your baby. Food should bring us together.

   This is not a step-by-step weaning guide. I don't believe that would be helpful for you or your baby. There are no schedules to follow here and no boxes to tick. Instead, I am hoping that the book will empower you to confidently make your own choices, based on what best suits you and your baby. As long as safe guidance is followed, you can watch and respond to your baby's cues. In this sense, *Intuitive Weaning* is a tailor-made, bespoke weaning approach.

A few myths to clear up...

The trouble with some weaning methods is that it is very easy for parents to fall into the trap of placing 'rule' above 'baby', particularly if you are lacking in confidence. Dogmatic approaches don't necessarily take into consideration the complex differences between babies.

   Babies eat best, and develop healthy relationships with food, when mealtimes feel calm and 'normal', so it is vital that your approach to weaning works for your family.

YOU DO NOT HAVE TO

- Track your baby's first 100 foods.
- Start with purée.
- Move through specific stages of texture.
- Offer a specific number of meals at any time.
- Follow a particular order of foods.
- Follow a milk/solids feeding schedule.
- Pick between Baby-led Weaning (BLW) and Traditional Weaning.
- Feel guilty for not managing to eat with your baby every day or cook from scratch every day.

IT IS ABSOLUTELY OK TO

- Spoon-feed your baby.
- Never spoon-feed your baby.
- Spoon-feed your baby when you/ they want to.
- Mix and match weaning styles.
- Give your baby the odd pouch of ready-made food.
- Never give your baby ready-made food.

My experience with popular weaning methods

You may have heard of the two main approaches to weaning. In a nutshell, Traditional Weaning methods generally suggest offering different textures in stages, beginning with purée, which is fed to the baby by a parent. Baby-led Weaning (BLW) – the term and approach coined by Dr Gill Rapley – focuses on a baby exclusively feeding themself from day one. Food is offered non-puréed and in the form of family meals that a baby will eat with their hands if they choose. The parent takes a big step back while the baby figures it out. The approach champions babies being in control of their own intake from the get-go and exploring food with all of their senses.

Being 'child-led'… means putting the interests and needs of the individual child at the forefront of adult decision-making

Teachers and nursery practitioners talk about 'child centredness' or of being 'child-led' all the time. It means putting the interests and needs of the individual child at the forefront of adult decision-making. In the same vein, being 'baby-led' has a similar meaning: *being led by your baby*. You can be 'baby-led' and not follow all of the Baby-led Weaning practical guidelines. In addition, being 'baby-led' will look very different from household to household, and even under the same roof.

Back in 2016, I took on Baby-led Weaning with my first daughter, Heidi, and it mostly suited her. I loved watching her feeding herself almost anything from the start. I extolled the benefits of Baby-led Weaning left, right and centre. I have the greatest of respect for Dr Gill Rapley. Her approach has led to an important shift away from 'parent in charge' to 'baby takes the lead', highlighting the importance of letting babies learn through discovery. However, two more babies down the line (and after many conversations with frustrated parents) I have come to the conclusion that the BLW approach in its purest form may not suit all babies and families.

With my second daughter, Nina, I found myself occasionally choosing to spoon-feed, which isn't really in-keeping with the original BLW method. This was for a combination of reasons – time saving on busy mornings, her own tiredness at dinner time and the fact she would sometimes just pass me the spoon! I didn't tell my

Instagram followers this for a while. I felt GUILTY about it. I felt as though I was lying to my followers. The situation was utterly ridiculous; I was responding to my baby's cues! I was BEING 'baby-led'! I wondered, *if my baby is giving me the spoon and 'asking' for help, what use is a 'hands-off' approach? What message does it send to her to refuse her wishes?* In my quest to go fully BLW, I was actually not being very baby-led.

Our surprise third baby, Felix, arrived in May 2020. When he began to eat, I decided to take my own approach to weaning. I let myself be truly led by him and led by the evidence. I also let myself be led by personal circumstance and convenience, with zero guilt for not cooking and zero guilt for rushed school-morning breakfasts of porridge via a spoon. It was a balance that worked for everyone. Felix and I preferred a mixture of self-feeding and spoon-feeding. Not once did I ever feel I wasn't being baby-led, that he wasn't getting enough hands-on food experience or receiving adequate nutrition. I realised that what really matters is keeping mealtime stress to an absolute minimum and aiming to make your baby's first experiences of food fun and exploratory. My experience with Felix was the first step in my mission to cut through the outdated debate between BLW and Traditional Weaning methods. I wanted to promote a simpler, judgement-free and far more child-centred approach: Intuitive Weaning.

Your baby just needs you

Intuitive Weaning is a culmination of so many things: my professional knowledge about how children learn and develop; my experience as a mother; my love of creating and sharing recipes; and my passion for helping babies and children to develop healthy attitudes towards food.

I hope this book helps you to enjoy the process of introducing food into your baby's diet, and enables you to see past the pressures of beautiful Instagram feeds and grumpy Facebook group mods. Your baby doesn't really need fancy blenders or the latest bamboo suction plates to start her weaning journey, regardless of what Instagram shows you. Your baby definitely doesn't need prescriptive rules or schedules. They just need you to watch, listen, respond and offer nutritious food.

Lastly, I truly hope your family enjoys my recipes. Each and every one has been cooked in 'real time' and tested by my own family, though I cannot guarantee they won't be thrown to the ground – that's babies for you!

Jo Weston

Note: The content of this book is not intended to replace medical advice. If you have concerns about your child's health, diet or development, always seek advice from a medical professional.

Before You Get Started

Well-informed parents know best

Well-informed parents know best. With that in mind, it's really important that you carefully read this chapter before you give your baby *any* food. All advice here is within NHS and the World Health Organization (WHO) guidance, accurate to date. If your baby has any health concerns, medical conditions or known allergies, seek professional medical advice before introducing solids.

What does the evidence say about different weaning approaches?

Baby-led Weaning has been linked to oral and fine motor development, less fussy eating and less overeating, although some critics suggest nutritional needs can be better met with Traditional Weaning. On the other hand, Traditional Weaning has drawn criticism for reducing a baby's exposure to different textures and tastes. The evidence points to pros and cons for both methods. This suggests that a more balanced, flexible approach may be the better way, with emphasis on self-feeding and offering highly nutritious foods. For some babies, this might be finger foods only; for others, a mix of smoother textures and finger foods.

When is the right time to introduce solids?

The WHO recommends that **babies begin to eat complementary foods at six months, as well as continuing to have milk feeds on demand.** Research suggests that exclusively milk-fed infants under six months are at less risk of gastrointestinal and respiratory infection, than babies who started solids at an earlier age. Breastmilk and formula milk offer far greater nutritional benefits than typical first foods (e.g. vegetable purées), therefore it makes sense to continue to exclusively breastfeed or formula feed for the first six months. At this age, the WHO advises introducing complementary foods to meet infants' growing need for nutrients, such as iron.

What are the signs that my baby is ready for solids?

Babies must be able to:

- Stay in a seated position, holding their head steady.
- Coordinate their eyes, hands and mouth, so they can look at their food, pick it up and put it in their mouth.
- Swallow food (rather than spit it back out).

These things tend to happen around the age of six months. Your baby does not need to be able to sit up completely independently – 'supported but steady' is perfectly fine. The key is to create a 'clear run' from mouth to stomach and ensure that your baby is sturdily grounded at the hip in order to minimise the risk of choking.

What about allergens?

You can introduce the common allergens below from six months. The advice is to offer them one at a time – one every few days will give enough time to spot any potential reactions. If you have a significant family history of allergy, it's worth discussing this with a health professional before you begin. It's also worth reading up on the different symptoms of food allergies, from mild to serious.

COMMON ALLERGENS

Cow's milk
(in cooking or mixed
with food)

Nuts and peanuts
(serve them crushed
or ground)

Shellfish
(don't serve raw
or lightly cooked)

Foods that
contain
gluten,
including
wheat, barley
and rye

Fish

Soya

Eggs
(eggs without a
British Lion stamp
should not be eaten
raw or lightly cooked)

Seeds
(serve them
crushed or
ground)

What are the best foods to offer my baby first?

There is some evidence to suggest that **babies need exposure to bitter, iron-rich greens earlier on** in order to avoid them relying too heavily on sweeter tastes later, but there's no need to delay the introduction of other foods once your baby is six months old. You may wish to offer just a few different kinds of roast or steamed veg in the first week, so you don't overwhelm your baby, but after that it is advisable to introduce some protein, grains, etc., too.

What can't I feed my baby?

The following should be avoided:

* **Sugary snacks** (sugar can cause tooth decay. You don't need to add sugar to your baby's food either. Many adults are conditioned to rely on sugar and salt for taste, but this is not the case for babies.)
* **Raw jelly cubes** (these can get stuck in the throat).
* **Whole nuts and peanuts** (these should not be given to children under five years old).
* **Honey** (avoid honey until your baby is 12 months old – it contains bacteria that can lead to infant botulism, a serious illness that can make your baby very unwell.)
* **Certain cheeses** (these can contain a bacteria called listeria. Avoid mould-ripened soft cheese, such as Brie or Camembert; ripened goat's milk cheese, such as chèvre; soft blue-veined cheese, such as Roquefort; and unpasteurised cheese.)
* **Raw shellfish** (this can increase the risk of food poisoning. Children should eat only shellfish that has been thoroughly cooked.)
* **Shark, swordfish or marlin** (high levels of mercury in these fish can affect your baby's growing nervous system).

A WORD ON SALT...

Too much salt can be harmful to your baby's developing kidneys, so it's best not to add salt to their meals. Babies are advised to have a maximum of 1g of salt per day, rising to 2g after 12 months, and 3g after 4 years. Some research has shown that babies who eat family foods from the beginning sometimes consume too much salt. I add lots of flavour to my recipes through, herbs, spices, garlic, fresh lemon, etc., but never salt. Feel free to season your own portion with salt, of course. It's also best to avoid foods that are high in salt, such as bacon, sausages, crisps, stock cubes and gravy. Serve foods like cheese and hummus in moderation, as these are salty, too.

Choosing when, and how often, to feed your baby

It doesn't matter which meal you choose to offer your baby first. As with all aspects of weaning, there are many variables here! I chose to include my babies every time I ate, if they wanted to, as it felt natural for them to be included at the dinner table. It's unlikely that your baby will overeat at this age. **Work meals in between your baby's usual milk times**, so that they are not over-hungry or completely full. Don't offer your baby food when they are getting tired as babies need to be alert in order to eat safely. Getting timings right can be tricky in the beginning, as your baby will still need regular naps and milk feeds, however you'll soon find a routine that works.

As the amount of solids your baby eats increases, their milk intake will slowly decrease. The NHS recommends that **babies should be eating three small meals a day by the time they turn one**. You may wish to encourage a milk drop towards the end of the first year if you feel your baby isn't eating enough. At **12 months a baby can drink cow's milk** if you wish them to, with a suggested maximum amount of 350ml a day.

Choking and gagging

Many parents worry about choking and rightfully so! It is important to be aware of foods that may be hazardous and to know how to prepare foods so that they are safe for your baby to eat. It is worth noting that research now shows that Baby-led Weaning, and eating 'finger foods' in general, does not increase a baby's risk of choking.

Gagging is actually very normal in the early days of solids. It's your baby's way of working out how much food they can process in one go and how to move it around their mouth. Babies have a strong gag reflex until around 9 months, so it is unlikely that they would swallow a large piece of food by accident. **When a baby gags on their food, you may notice they screw up their face, cough, have watery eyes or are even sick**. Baby will usually be absolutely fine after a gagging episode. Never try to get food out of a baby's mouth if they are gagging, as that may cause them to choke. Stay calm and reassure them.

If a baby is choking, they will be silent and will not be able to breathe. It is rare, but of course it happens, and I really recommend taking a baby first aid course so you are prepared if the worst were to happen.

SNACKS

Babies under one generally do not need snacks. Their meals and milk feeds are usually enough. Snacks marketed at babies under one are fine to serve alongside a meal, but it's better that they 'snack' on breastmilk or formula at that age.

COMMON CHOKING HAZARDS

Cherry tomatoes

&

Whole grapes
(both must always
be quartered)

Cylindrical foods
like hot dog sausages
(cut these lengthways
through the middle)

Thickly spread
peanut butter

Whole
nuts

Hard, round
foods, like
boiled sweets

Raw carrot

Popcorn

Raw apple

What equipment do I need?

Not a lot really! I recommend...

- **A highchair;** ideally wipe clean and with a footrest for stability.
- **Bibs;** both long-sleeve and scoop styles.
- **Open cups** are best for oral development as they encourage tipping upwards and sipping, rather than a sucking action; use a free-flow sippy cup for taking out and about.
- **Cutlery;** chunky and soft for beginners; toddler metal cutlery from around one year old.
- **Plates and bowls;** styles with a suction base can be useful.

(For younger babies you may find it easier to put food straight on the highchair tray.)

... and a good broom!

Vitamins and minerals

It is recommended that **all children from six months are given vitamin A, C and D supplements**. These are the vitamins that babies and young children sometimes struggle to get enough of through diet alone. Babies who are breastfed should be given Vitamin D from birth (formula-fed babies will already be getting enough from their formula). By six months, iron stores have begun to diminish, so it is important to include iron-rich foods, such as red meat, leafy green vegetables, nut butters and pulses in your baby's diet, as well as foods rich in Vitamin C, which help your baby to process iron.

Water

Babies need to drink water with meals to avoid constipation. In the UK, tap water doesn't have to be boiled after your baby turns six months old, so water straight from the tap is fine.

Spoon-feeding responsively

Porridge, yoghurt, soups, risottos, curries with rice... it's OK to let baby give these foods a go with their hands (and you would be amazed what they manage), but you may choose to spoon-feed, too. Here are some tips:

- Have **multiple spoons** available so that your baby can have a go at feeding themself.
- **Load up spoons** ready and see if they will bring them to their mouth.
- **Give your baby lots of time** to finish each mouthful.
- **Talk to your baby** about each bite so they knows what they are eating.
- Offer some **finger food** alongside the spoon-fed meal, if you can.
- Swap between feeding your baby and letting them feed themself. **Let your baby have a go**, then offer help if they get frustrated or tired.
- **Never worry about finishing a portion of food**, even if there really is 'just one more bite'. If your baby has had enough, the meal needs to end.

Serving first foods safely

While many elements of starting solids are flexible, there is a 'right' way to safely prep first foods to avoid the risk of choking. Before giving food to your baby, you need to make sure that it adheres to the following safety points:

- Food must be **soft enough** to squash between your thumb and finger.
- Food must be around the **length and width of an adult's index finger**, or in a piece bigger than your baby's fist.
- **Seeds and pips must be removed.**
- Some **fruit and vegetable skins will need removing.** If the skin won't easily disintegrate (like courgette) or if it slips off the food easily (like on soft fruit), then it is best to discard. Leaving thicker, secure skin as a 'handle' on foods such as cucumber, melon and mango is fine.
- **Pieces of food must not be placed in a baby's mouth** by anyone other than the baby.
- **Small pieces should be avoided** until your baby is able to pick them up, as they are much harder for your baby to navigate safely in their mouth.

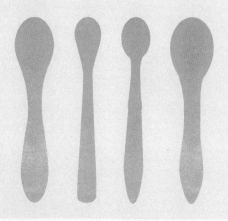

This chart should give you an idea of how to serve food safely to your baby, from six months:

FRUITS

Raspberries
Just open them out.

Blueberries*
Squash or cut in half.

Grapes*
Cut in quarters. Continue to cut grapes until your child is around five.

Blackberries*
Quarter lengthways due to their tough core.

Strawberries
Very large strawberries (bigger than your baby's fist) can be cut in half. Smaller ones need chopping.

Banana
If you gently squeeze, it will break lengthways into thirds perfect for babies to hold.

Apples
Bake until soft. Older babies with plenty of teeth may manage thinly sliced raw apple.

Oranges
Cut big slices, removing any pips. Bigger oranges are more suitable than little tangerines. If you do give tangerines, remove the middle membrane to 'burst' them.

Tomatoes
Big slices of beef tomatoes or large vine tomatoes are perfect. Once babies have developed their pincer grip, they can have quartered cherry tomatoes*.

cucumber — sticks

blueberries — smashed

grapes — quarters

avocado — long wedge

broccoli — large floret

sweet potato — long wedge

chicken — long strip

orange — big slice

* Some foods are tricky for babies to hold until they've developed a pincer grip (see page 31). These are safe to serve from six months if prepared as described, but your baby may struggle to pick them up until a little later.

VEGETABLES

Broccoli
A large floret as big as
your baby's hand.

Green beans
Serve whole but slightly
overcooked.

Leafy greens
Chop finely into meals
or blend.

Courgette
Chop into sticks and roast
or stir-fry.

Peppers
Roast and then peel until
baby can handle the skin.

Sweet potato
Slice into wedges and
roast or mash.

Aubergine
Slice into wedges and
roast or stir-fry.

Avocado
Slice into long wedges.

Cucumber
Cut into batons, leaving
a little skin for grip.

CARBOHYDRATES

Potatoes
Make your own chips
(without salt of course),
make mash (ideal to eat
with hands) or scoop out
the middle of a jacket
potato.

Rice and couscous
You can spoon-feed these.
Offer on loaded spoons or
combine with mashed root
veg and roll into balls.

Pasta
Bigger shapes such as
fusilli gigante, are best.
Otherwise opt for long
spaghetti, smaller fusilli
or baby pasta. It's best to
overcook until completely
soft.

Bread
Minimise as it contains
salt. Best to lightly toast
in the beginning. White
grains are advised over
wholegrain, as wholegrain
can fill up a baby's tummy
too much. A small amount
of brown bread is fine if
that's your family's usual
loaf.

PROTEIN

Red meat
Slow-cooked or minced is
best, but it's fine to give
strips of steak or pork
chop to a toothless baby
to suck on. Once baby has
a tooth, stick to softer,
more manageable meats.

White meat
Roast or marinated
chicken is best. Opt for
long, soft pieces or shred.
Turkey mince is a good,
too.

Fish
Fish is softer and easier
than meat. Cut finger-
sized pieces from a larger
cooked fillet, following
the natural lines where
the fish flakes.

Tinned beans
Mash and roll into a ball
that baby can pick up.
Small beans are great for
pincer grip practice.

Yoghurt
Thick, full-fat yoghurt is
fairly easy for a baby to
pick up with their hands
or you can take turns with
a spoon.

Eggs
Slice hard-boiled eggs
into quarters, snip
omelettes into strips and
cook scrambled egg into
clumps.

Nut butter
Spread thinly on toast
or banana, or stir into
porridge. Never give
spoonfuls of nut butter to
a baby.

Cheese
Grated or included in
cooking is safest. As
babies gain control they
will be able to handle
thin slices.

Babies are incredible at eating intuitively. They are born to do so!

My Intuitive Weaning approach

Intuitive Weaning is my own approach to introducing complementary foods (or 'weaning'). I have developed this philosophy as a result of my own frustrations with current guidance, my passion for helping families to eat happily and my knowledge of how babies learn. It is not a prescriptive 'method', but it is guidance that you can tailor to the needs of your family. My hope is that it will help you to follow your baby's lead with confidence and understanding.

The word 'intuitive' has two different implications here:

1 Following your own intuition when offering solids to your baby.

2 Allowing your baby to respond to their natural instincts when they are eating.

I am greatly inspired by Evelyn and Tribole's Intuitive Eating philosophy. It rejects diet mentality and promotes **reconnecting with the body to truly recognise hunger and fullness**. It encourages people to learn to trust themselves to eat what they need and to truly enjoy food. Babies are incredible at eating intuitively. They are born to do so! Shortly after birth, and if given the chance, babies instinctively crawl up to their mother's breast for their first ever feed. They feed until full and then they usually fall asleep until woken again by hunger. **They are born with the innate ability to signal for food when hungry and to stop when full.** Babies *know* how to eat. Many adults, however, have forgotten. Frequently adults restrict their food or over-eat because of boredom or comfort. They either purposefully ignore feelings of hunger or never let themselves feel it at all.

Diet culture has a lot to answer for. It creates a disconnect between our body's needs and our choices around food. Sadly, this seems increasingly the case for our children's relationship with food, too. Something goes astray on the path between babyhood and late childhood, and eating is frequently way out of sync by adulthood. We stop trusting our bodies. Babies need us to trust that they can respond to their own hunger. We mustn't undermine this by encouraging them to eat less or more than they wish to. Let's give them the best start we can so that they continue to eat intuitively – starting with weaning!

KEY PRINCIPLES

To shape my approach to weaning, I have broken it down into what I feel are the most important elements:

Respect, responsiveness and realism

Cooking, eating and enjoying

Letting your baby play with their food

Following safe (science-based) guidance

Respect

I believe that babies are so much more complex than cute sponges that soak up new information. For example, new research shows that **newborn babies have an innate understanding of the laws of physics**, so they are hardly 'empty vessels'! Babies deserve our respect, in everything, and should be given the same treatment and rights as any other person. This has implications for every area of parenting, including weaning. Offering solids respectfully looks similar to serving an adult a beautiful meal. It *doesn't* look like putting petrol in the car. To put it less bluntly, **respectful weaning is more about including your baby at the table** and helping them to feel comfortable around food than it is about the task of filling an empty tummy.

By about six months, babies begin to realise that they are a separate person to you. They begin to develop their personalities. Those cries of protest when you move away from a game, giggles in the build-up to peek-a-boo are all ways a baby shows their **new-found self-awareness**. This is a really important time to show that we respect and understand their feelings and preferences. Introducing solids at six months gives babies lots of opportunities to make real

choices. Carrot or broccoli first? More, or no more? **Letting your baby make these choices will help them to build confidence** and will show them that you are listening.

Respecting appetites and food choices (even if it means that greens go uneaten sometimes) makes children feel safe around food. To begin, you could offer just one or two pieces of food, offering more if your baby shows interest. This simple act is the first step in respecting your baby's decisions around food. Babies find ways to tell us that they have finished their meal – shaking their head, throwing their bowl, clamping their mouth shut. You can respect your baby's choice not to eat something with a smiley 'all finished?' and

'Respecting a child means treating even the youngest infant as a unique human being, not as an object'
MAGDA GERBER

removing their food. Here-comes-the-aeroplane-style feeding and tricking toddlers into eating their veg have no place here!

What does 'respect' look like when starting solids?	How do I do this?
Recognising that your baby is their own person.	Encourage your baby to self-feed when they are ready.
Encouraging choice.	Give options from day one. This is as simple as your baby choosing to taste what you offer, or not!
Including your baby at the dinner table.	Have family mealtimes (when you can); talk to your baby during dinner; put phones away.
Never overriding a baby or child's choice about food.	It is their choice whether to eat something. You should *never* force or bribe your child to eat.

Responsiveness

Prior to the introduction of solids, the NHS advises that **parents should breastfeed or bottle feed responsively, watching closely for signs of hunger and fullness.** This should naturally cross over into introducing solids and continue well into childhood. It is more important to be responsive to a baby's personal preferences than it is to stick to a schedule or to an approach with strict rules.

There's no need to choose between Baby-led Weaning and Traditional Weaning if they don't quite suit your baby (fine if they do). If your baby is clearly feeling frustrated with eating a certain food with their hands, it's OK to help with a spoon. On the flipside, if you are choosing to spoon-feed and your baby is refusing, try letting them feed themself with their hands. If your baby is teething and only wanting yoghurt and fruit, give them yoghurt and fruit for a while. If your baby is feeling poorly and preferring milk feeds, go with it. The first year of food is important for exposure to flavours and textures, practising the practical skills of eating and developing positive attitudes towards food. While what we offer our babies nutritionally is very important, variety being key, it is also so important that we try to keep our babies happy and calm in any eating situation. You can lead a horse to water but you can't make it drink.

> *The key is to watch. This is how we listen to babies.*

The key is to watch. This is how we listen to babies. When your baby was born, you learnt to recognise when they were hungry, tired or overstimulated. You will learn their cues around eating solids too; their likes and dislikes, satiety (fullness), and frustrations. There may be challenging and confusing moments as you begin to offer food to your baby. Even with my third baby it took me a while to figure out the best times to eat and what to offer when. It really is a case of watching, trying and watching again... and a little bit of guesswork, too!

Parental responsiveness in feeding has been linked to **reducing the likelihood of your baby becoming overweight or developing disordered eating further down the line.** It is easy to second-guess a baby's hunger if they haven't eaten much, or be keen for them to finish the last spoonful of dinner, but it is so important that we try to override these impulses. Even if there really is only one more bite to go, if your baby has finished, let them be finished. No pressure.

What does 'responsiveness' look like when starting solids?	How do I do this?
Recognising when your baby is ready to start solids.	Look for the signs of readiness (see page 31) and understanding that there is no particular date to begin (around six months doesn't mean six months on the dot).
Continuing to offer milk feeds on demand at first.	To begin, offer solids between milk feeds, when a baby is likely to be neither overly hungry or completely full up.
Watching and responding to signs of interest.	Watch your baby exploring the food, in very small amounts at first. Let them pick it up, squash it, smell it, taste it… whatever they need to do! You can offer more if they enjoy this experience.
Watching and responding to signs of discomfort.	Your baby may not react positively, may become upset or just refuse to engage with the food. That's OK. Take your baby out and reassure them. Try again later.
Watching and responding to signs that your baby is full up.	Your baby may turn their head, clamp their mouth shut (more likely if being spoon-fed), throw their food, wriggle in their seat or cry. You may recognise your baby has their very own signs, too.
Not offering food to soothe or placate a baby.	Avoid offering food to distract a crying baby as it won't help them to eat intuitively.
Placing 'baby above book'.	Abandon a strict feeding schedule, weaning approach or meal plan if you or your baby are not happy. Feed your baby how *they* prefer to be fed.

Realism

It's hard to predict how your baby will respond when you start to offer solids. Some babies happily dive straight in, but others take a little longer. Some are easily overwhelmed and may find the whole experience just too much, others find certain sensations tricky to process and some just take longer to actually eat the food they are presented with. I have spoken with many parents whose babies took a while to 'get going' – it's completely normal!

I receive a lot of messages sent in frustration from parents wondering why their baby suddenly won't eat or why their toddler is now insistent on having their food separated. Almost all of the time the causes of these behaviours are developmentally normal and to be expected – it is our own expectations and reactions that can be the most challenging to overcome. Understanding what to expect will help you to feel confident and accept that weaning isn't always plain sailing or linear.

There is a lot of pressure on parents to do and be everything for their children. Being realistic also refers to yourself. **A positive introduction to food does not mean that you have to spend hours in the kitchen.** The recipes in this book are simple, straightforward and suitable for everyone, meaning that you don't

What does 'being realistic' look like when starting solids?	How do I do this?
Recognising that babies will have times when their appetites dip.	Begin to understand why and when this might happen in order to help you to stay calm and ride through it. Let go of any expectations of your baby so that you can more easily go with the flow.
Recognising that Instagram-perfect family meals are not always the reality.	Accept that real life gets in the way and learn that being 'good enough' is more than enough for your baby.
Managing the new task of preparing suitable meals for your baby.	Plan your meals. Keep it simple. Adapt the recipes you already know and learn a few new ones, too!

have to cook twice (unless eating separately is more suited to your family arrangements). Not all meals need to be cooked completely from scratch either. There are even some brilliant nutritionist-led baby-suitable ready meals available for days when things go to pot or you just need a break from cooking. Dinner time may not always be the whole family sitting around the table happily eating the same home-cooked meal. That may sometimes be the reality, but it's fine if it isn't always. With a young family of five, I know very well that differing bedtimes, emotional needs and parental work commitments can make a shared meal difficult to achieve every single day. We do our best and compromise by ensuring that, at the very least, no one eats alone.

It is our own expectations and reactions that can be the most challenging to overcome

Letting Your Baby Play With Their Food

For babies, a big part of developing a relationship with food comes from exploring it with all five senses. **Babies learn about food, and from food, through play.** There is so much to say about this and it's useful for you to know *why* it is so great that your baby is covered in spaghetti and meatballs – this will also help you see past the mess! The next chapter is devoted to exploring your baby's development in relation to food.

Cooking, Eating & Enjoying

How we eat and our attitudes towards food are very important for our babies. We are role models. Babies have been watching us eat since they were born. **Babies learn a lot through observing adults and imitating them** (this is called Modelling Theory). It's a good idea to eat how we want our babies to eventually eat; at the table, seated, eating a range of foods, using cutlery where required and chatting positively. This is actually quite a lot harder than you might think! As a busy mum, I find myself fighting the temptation to wolf down a slice of toast as I empty the dishwasher while my kids eat at the table. We all do it! But as a general rule, it's really helpful for our babies to see us stop, sit and enjoy a balanced meal, even if for just one meal a day.

A NOTE ON SUPPORTING YOUR BABY
IF YOU HAVE A POOR RELATIONSHIP
WITH FOOD

It can be challenging to encourage your baby to eat a range of foods if you have a limited diet yourself. It's fine to have dislikes and to talk about them, but watching a parent trying new foods will help a baby to do the same. Perhaps you could try some of the new foods with your baby, in similar amounts. This will help your baby to learn that they are 'safe' foods. Don't put too much pressure on yourself to change your entire diet; just take small steps.

Many of us have emotional baggage around food, myself included. If you can, try to see weaning as a clean slate for yourself – an opportunity to move on from past battles of yoyo dieting or under/overeating. I know that weaning can be a trigger for those who have previously suffered eating disorders, leading to worries about the amount babies are eating or concern over whether they are fostering a healthy diet and attitude for their baby. Many parents have reached out to me about this, knowing that I, too, have suffered from eating disorders

in the past. If this resonates with you, know that you *are* capable of feeding your baby well. This may be a good time to seek some extra support for any emotional battles you have around food – it's never too late and it may help to end the cycle of disordered thinking around food.

In terms of cooking, weaning can feel a little bit daunting for 'non-cooks', but I really believe that there is no need to overcomplicate the food you cook and serve to your baby. I also don't believe it is necessary to cook separate meals for babies unless you wish to. All my recipes are suitable for the whole family. Flavour is maximised through careful and plentiful combinations of herbs, spices, citrus, garlic ... just not salt and sugar! And, trust me, you quickly learn to adapt your palate and your cooking to be free from added sugar and salt. If your baby sees you eating and enjoying the same food that they have in front of them, this will send them all of the right messages.

Following safe guidance

There is much space for flexibility in the hows and whats of introducing solids. As long as you are clued up on key guidance and you are following your baby's lead, you will be getting it right.

To conclude this chapter... YOU CAN DO THIS! The number of meals you offer at first, the foods you introduce first, whether you eat all your meals together or just some, whether you spoon-feed or choose not to – these are all *choices* that you can make based on what you feel is best for your baby and what you personally feel comfortable with. Follow the science, follow your baby, follow your intuition and enjoy these precious first meals together. That is my key advice for calm and straightforward weaning.

The language of eating

It's really important to be mindful of the words we use around food. I'm a firm believer that there are no 'good' or 'bad' foods. We are not 'good' or 'bad' for choosing to eat or not eat something. Eating up all my dinner does not make me a good person; it makes me a hungry one!

The same goes for babies. It's best to keep our language around food neutral as our babies will slowly pick up on our words and body language.

Here are some food-neutral phrases you could adopt if you find yourself slipping into these 'old-school' phrases.

I'd advise sharing this with any family member who may be caring for your little one as attitudes change from generation to generation. It's good to check that everyone is on the same page.

Instead of...
'Here comes the aeroplane!'

Try...
'You're shaking your head, you don't want any more of this do you?'

Instead of...
'Oh no! You bumped your arm! Let's have a biscuit to make you feel better.'

Try...
'Oh no! You bumped your arm! Let's have a cuddle to make you feel better.'

Instead of...
'One more bite for Mummy? There's only one bit left!'

Try...
'All finished? That's OK.'

Instead of...
'Yucky, you HATE spinach don't you!'

Try...
'Not keen on that one? Maybe next time.'

Instead of...
'Good girl for eating it all up!'

Try...
'Looks like you were hungry today!' or 'Wow! You used your spoon all by yourself!'

Learning to eat

(and why it's OK to play with your food!)

Coming from a background in education, I am continuously fascinated by how babies and young children learn, and how a child's early experiences can shape their entire lives. Our interactions with food are nutritionally important, but also they aid a baby's development and, importantly, help to secure positive relationships with food. Understanding just a little bit about typical child development can help us to support our babies to learn to eat and can help us to get through common meal time frustrations!

Timeline of skills needed to eat solids, from birth to 12 months

As they develop, babies acquire certain skills that are needed in order to eat. This timeline will give you an idea of the developmental lead-up to eating solids and the progression thereafter.

Please remember that **the ages on this timeline are approximate** – babies develop at their own pace.

The timeline gives a picture of where your baby started, where they may be now, and where they are going. I find it really interesting that babies suckle and swallow by reflex but appear to have to learn to munch and chew! You can see how **at six months most babies have developed the skills needed to bring food to their mouths by themselves,** meaning that they can now safely begin to eat.

Babies learn by exploring the world through their senses and bodies

Age	Skill
BIRTH TO 1 MONTH	Baby is born with rooting and suckling reflexes, will push food out of their mouth (tongue-thrust reflex), cry when hungry and bring hands to mouth.
2 MONTHS	Baby begins to hold their head up and open and shut their hands.
3 MONTHS	Baby builds enough strength in their hands to hold a toy.
4 MONTHS	Baby begins to hold their head steady, reach for objects (grasping with their palms) and chew on objects.
5 MONTHS	Baby begins to sit, with support.
6 MONTHS	Baby begins to sit on their own, hold things with two hands and drop objects.
7 MONTHS	Baby begins to learn to chew; baby may have a few teeth.
8 MONTHS	Baby begins to pass objects or food from one hand to another.
9 MONTHS	Baby begins to pick up smaller objects using pincer grip.
10 MONTHS	Baby's gag reflex begins to mature; baby may begin to point to foods.
11 MONTHS	Baby may be able to feed themselves with a spoon.
12 MONTHS	Baby may begin to express themselves verbally at mealtimes – 'no', 'more', etc.

The benefits of a hands-on approach to introducing solids

Babies learn by exploring the world through their senses and bodies (The Swiss Psychologist Piaget called this the 'Sensorimotor Stage'). They learn by playing and doing, learning rapidly with each action they make. While this process of learning is natural, we can aid a baby's natural curiosity and active learning by offering sensory experiences. By offering your baby a range of colourful foods in a range of textures daily, you are doing wonders for their brain development!

Offering food in its original form helps babies to make connections between how their food looks, smells, tastes, feels and even sounds. Consider the differences in the eating experience between purée and unblended foods.

Offering food in its whole form may also help your baby to recognise and accept it, particularly if it is offered regularly. If a food is always blended with another, it can be harder to recognise the individual flavours.

As well as being beneficial for a baby's cognitive development, **giving your baby lots of self-feeding practice will help them to build up fine and gross motor skills.** These same skills will eventually be used for scribbling, then drawing, then (much later!) writing. Squeezing a large orange segment, swinging long lengths of spaghetti, clawing at muffins, splashing sauces and learning to hold on tight to that slippery veg stick are all excellent workouts for hand and arm muscles. Understanding this may also help you to accept a little bit of inevitable mess!

Puréed chicken & vegetables

Roast chicken dinner

Puréed: One sound.

Whole: Baby can hear the slight difference in sound when they eat foods of differing textures – squeaks, crunches, swallows, etc.

Puréed: Brown.

Whole: Orange carrots, green broccoli, shiny peas, textured chicken.

Puréed: Not a lot to feel, if spoon-fed.

Whole: Bobbly broccoli, smooth carrots, lumpy mash, stringy chicken, rolling peas. What happens when I squash, throw, pinch, squeeze this food?

Puréed: One taste.

Whole: Tasting each individual component.

Puréed: One smell.

Whole: savoury chicken, fresh vegetables, mouth-watering roast potatoes.

Changing grip

When you begin introducing solids, your baby will probably be using a palmar grasp (holding things in their palm). This means that you need to offer babies food that they can grip in this way. Chunky and long, or fist-sized, items are perfect, providing the food is soft enough to eat with few, or no, teeth. This will help your baby to be successful when self-feeding, which will help them to build confidence. It is also much safer as your baby will have increased control. Soon, you may also notice your baby develops a 'raking' action, clawing things towards themselves with their fingers.

As your baby gets older, the way they pick up food will change. From around eight months (but often later), you can begin to give your baby much smaller pieces so that they can practise their developing pincer grip. Give a mixture of larger ('grabbable') pieces and small pieces at first to avoid frustration. Once they are confidently picking up the small pieces you can serve all of their food cut small until they are able to use a knife and fork (though this won't be until they are much, much older).

Piaget believed that babies learn new concepts through repeated patterns of behaviour, called 'schema'. For example, a baby with a 'trajectory' schema may take great joy in repeatedly dropping food from their highchair. It's useful to know that there are good reasons why babies do these (sometimes annoying!) things.

Using cups

It's a good idea to introduce a small, open cup from the beginning, as it is preferable for your baby's oral and dental development. They may need your support to hold the cup at first, but it's surprising how quickly babies learn to hold and sip from a cup. Sippy cups and water bottles are best saved for when you are out and about or in a bit of a rush.

As your baby enters toddlerhood, I recommend using small, durable glass tumblers (the kind you used to get at school). We introduced a glass of this sort from around ten months with Felix, following the Montessori-based idea that **giving children real items helps them to handle everyday objects with care, confidence and increased spatial awareness.** For the same reason, I recommend introducing ceramic plates as soon as you can. Even very young children can learn to handle cups and plates carefully when they are given the responsibility to do so.

FOOD PLAY

Some babies take a little longer to feel comfortable with handling and tasting food. If this is the case, have a go with some of these simple sensory activities:

* **Yoghurt paint.** Plain yoghurt coloured with berries. You can add cutlery or brushes if you like.

* **Purée paint.** Let your baby dip their fingers in, and paint a tray.

* **Blackberry paint:** Give your baby a few blackberry halves and a large piece of paper taped to the floor. Let them create a masterpiece!

* **Cooked spaghetti.** You can add a tiny amount of food colouring if you wish. Great for wiggling and squishing.

* **Cooked porridge.** Add farm animals or diggers.

* **Cereal play** (for babies with teeth). Use to scoop, stack, mix or use as pretend animal feed.

* **Citrus fruit water play.** Slice oranges, lemons, grapefruit and limes, and float them in a tray of water. Your baby will love to taste and squeeze the fruit and splash the water.

* **Warm and cold.** Fill two clear water bottles with warm and icy water. Let your baby explore the temperature difference, talking about them as they play.

* **Fruit and vegetable treasure basket.** This is great for introducing new foods. Try butternut squash, sweet potato, broccoli, big salad leaves, pineapple, watermelon, coconut, kiwi, bananas ... you can chop into them to explore what's inside, too!

* **Herb sniffing.** Keep old herb pots for baby to sniff or wrap herbs in secured muslin cloths or socks.

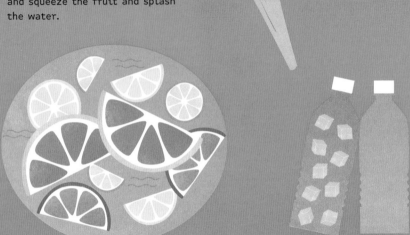

Into toddlerhood

Happy birthday! Over the last six months, your baby has moved through the stages of first tastes and sensory exploration and has developed many new skills. It's likely your baby (who is quickly growing into a toddler) eats three meals a day now, plus a couple of snacks and a couple of milk feeds. You may even find you have a lovely honeymoon period where your little one is growing in confidence with eating, maintaining a routine and mostly eating what you cook for them – hooray!

At around 18 months you may notice a few changes in eating habits and preferences. This, combined with growing independence and communication is often when parents begin to feel a little more challenged. It's good to know what to expect as your baby transitions into a toddler, so you can work with their 'new normal' rather than fight against it.

Power struggles

The toddler stage can be overwhelming and frustrating for both parent and child. Toddlers have this new 'all by my own' sense of independence and yet don't always have the freedom or control that they wish for. Equally, they still need so much comfort and support to help them with the many new emotions they can now experience. It's tough being a toddler! Mealtimes become an easy target for power struggles.

How do we cope with this? Try to keep in mind the three R's of Intuitive Weaning from chapter 2: respect, responsiveness and realism.

❶ Respect

Continue to listen and respect when your child says they don't want to eat something. No bribery, no negotiating.

❷ Responsiveness

Why is your child suddenly refusing food or fussing? Are they actually tired or bored? Are they looking for more attention, connection or control?

❸ Realism

This is normal. Your child may well be working out how to assert themselves or experiencing common toddler food aversions.

It can be so painful to lovingly cook a meal for your child only for them to push it away, run off or say, 'not like it, mummy;' especially when they ate it happily as a baby. I have

> ## 'Trust your child to eat the amount that is right for her'
> ELLYN SATTER

been there so many times and it can be hard to know how to react. Your head is saying, 'that can't possibly be enough,' or 'I can't let my child only eat ice cream.' It is easy to panic and slip into *one more pea and then you can have your pudding* territory, but this can compound emotional eating behaviours. Extensive research into 'fussy eating' shows that pressuring children to eat simply makes the problem worse, so don't undo all the amazing work you did when weaning. Below are a few tried-and-tested toddler tips to help you navigate stressful mealtimes. I have used all of these strategies myself.

'Snacks!'

If I had a penny for every time I hear that word in my house! From one year old, it is advised that toddlers have two small snacks a day between meals in order to meet their energy requirements. However, many, many toddlers ask for more than this. Try planning your snack times and offering something that will sustain your child until the next mealtime. Worried your toddler is over-snacking? Grazing all day makes it harder for children to build a proper appetite for meals.

Remember, at this age, children are still learning what the different sensations in their bodies mean and how to verbalise how their bodies are feeling. My second daughter would (and sometimes still does) confuse hunger with tiredness. If your little one asks for snacks a lot, try to check in with them. Are they thirsty, tired or bored? Sometimes distraction can help you to work out whether your child is *actually* hungry or not.

Ellyn Satter's Division of Responsibility (sDOR)

As your toddler gets older, I recommend looking into *The Division of Responsibility*. I am a huge fan of Ellyn's approach. Sometimes as a parent you just want to feel as though you have control over a situation. sDOR will help you feel in control while still fully respecting your child. The general principles are that parents decide when eating times will be (with consideration for the child's age, needs and hunger) and what will be served (with consideration for the child's preferences). The child decides whether to eat and how much. The approach is simple but incredibly powerful.

Ellyn believes that family meals and *enjoying* food are important for helping children to develop healthy eating habits and attitudes towards food. As a parent, I find that sticking to my jobs of deciding when, where and what to eat stops me from interfering with my children's job of deciding how much they eat. No bribery, no pleading.

However, there needs to be great flexibility for babies and young toddlers who will not yet understand the concept of waiting for a meal or snack time at all (and it would be unrealistic to expect them to do so without tears). Your job of deciding when to offer food can be as flexible as you need it to be, based on the needs, age and understanding of your child. For example, an 18-month-old toddler may not eat lunch, but may ask for food half an hour later. It would be unfair to expect her to wait another hour until snack time.

IDEAS FOR BALANCED SNACKS

Fruit:
- with nut butter
- with cheese

Rice cakes with avocado and banana

½ slice of wholemeal toast with butter and marmite

Berries and yoghurt

A savoury or fruit muffin or scone (see pages 182–188 for recipes)

Banana bread

Cucumber sticks and hummus

CHILD'S JOB

Choosing whether they eat; how much they eat.

PARENT'S JOB

Choosing when to eat; where to eat; what to serve; **Preparing the food.**

Typical toddler mealtimes challenges, explained

Getting down from the table
and running off before the meal has finished.

WHY?

They maybe exploring new-found freedom from the highchair or they may have just reached their 'sitting limit' (two-year-olds, for example, can often stay seated at an activity for only 5–10 minutes, sometimes less).

WHAT DO I DO ABOUT IT?!

- **Lower your expectations.**
- **Praise them for joining** you at the table when they first sit down and as they leave the table.
- **Keep them engaged** by involving them in the chat as much as you can.
- **Check they are actually comfortable** at the table and that they can reach.

- -

Refusing to eat foods they ate before.

WHY?

It may be a case of food neophobia: the fear of trying new foods. Studies show this is common in toddlers. If they won't eat something they previously enjoyed, it may be because they have no memory of eating it when they were younger, so it becomes a new food again.

WHAT DO I DO ABOUT IT?!

- **Offer**, but don't force or pressurise.
- **Always make sure there is something available that they do enjoy.**
- **Try serving buffet-style**, from the middle of the table.
- **Don't hide vegetables** as it won't help to build trust and can actually reinforce fears around new foods.

- -

Eating only certain foods ('just pasta!') in certain ways
('no sauce!') on certain plates ('no, blue plate!').

WHY?

Toddlers who seem demanding are often just desperate to have a little more control in their lives.

WHAT DO I DO ABOUT IT?!

- **Always let them have the blue plate/ pink cup**, even if it isn't convenient. It's a small thing to you, but choices like this are a really big deal to toddlers.
- **Give them some control away from the table** – what they wear, what they play with, where they go.
- **Give them some control at the table.** Let them choose which fruit they would like, let them serve themselves at dinner (with help). Let them choose which parts of the meal they eat.

Liking only plain food.

WHY?

It's very normal for toddlers to go through a 'beige phase', even if they have been exposed to a range of exciting foods as a baby. Toddlers like familiarity – it's comforting for them.

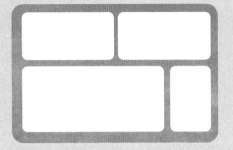

WHAT DO I DO ABOUT IT?!

● **Switch up how you offer the main course.** Divided plates can be less overwhelming for toddlers, as they can see and more easily choose what they are eating.

● **Try separating meals** such as stir fries and salads into separate components.

● **Offer vegetables and sauces on the side**, so that they become a choice.

● **Keep cooking and offering a range of foods** to the whole family, as this will help to normalise them.

● **Try serving all the food from the table**, including items that you know your child likes. Make no mention of any part of the meal being 'theirs' or 'mine'.

- -

Only wanting dessert.

WHY?

Toddlers often have a preference for sweeter foods, particularly if social cues have led them to begin to think of sweeter foods as special. Also, dessert is often more familiar than the main course. Many toddlers would choose the familiar pot of fromage frais (which is always exactly the same) over a meal with lots of different components.

WHAT DO I DO ABOUT IT?!

● **Offer dessert even if the main meal is unfinished.** This helps to prevent dessert being seen as the 'holy grail' and can help to ensure that your little one's dietary needs are being met.

● **Try offering dessert alongside the main meal.** This instantly eliminates the battle, as it is now up to the toddler to decide the order in which they eat their meal. You would be surprised at how much of the main meal will still be eaten – I promise!

● **Keep desserts as nutritious as possible** – ideally low sugar, containing fruit and some dairy. All the dessert recipes in this book are perfect for toddlers!

● **Try to avoid language such as 'treat' or 'naughty food'.** This reinforces that there is something special about cakes/chocolate/desserts and just makes it more desirable. It's best to put them on a level playing field.

Offering alternatives

I believe there is a balance to be struck here. If I cook a new recipe and one of my children doesn't like it, I offer them something else. An adult may go to the kitchen and make a sandwich in that scenario, but a toddler cannot do that. It's unfair (and not very respectful) to expect them to eat a meal that they do not like. If I cook a meal that I *know* they would usually eat, I presume they just aren't that hungry and no alternative is given, though I may make an exception if they are feeling particularly emotional or they are poorly. Dessert is always offered, regardless of how much dinner is eaten, as that is part of our family meal (and never regarded as a reward). A small snack is offered right before bed if anyone is hungry.

Why I don't do 'here comes the aeroplane' or hidden/ sneaky veg

We all know that toddlers are not stupid. It's very important that our toddlers can trust us and that we respect them enough to be honest about what we are feeding them. Hiding food in other foods, whether we reveal it at the end or not, is simply tricking your child into eating something. Hiding spinach in a dish only for your child to find it and be shocked and repulsed is a sure-fire way to put them off both spinach and, possibly, your cooking in general!

If we want to raise 'intuitive eaters', we mustn't slip into commonly used bribery and coercion to get our children to eat, no matter how much we want them to finish (or start!) their meal. Eating for stickers, treats or dessert is not intuitive eating. In fact, it actively encourages children to ignore their hunger cues, eat beyond fullness and view some foods as more preferable to others (e.g. a slice of chocolate cake offered if the carrots get eaten is seen by the child as the 'prize'). If your child doesn't want to eat their greens or finish their meal, put on your well-practised poker face, move the conversation along and try again next time. Your relaxed approach will pay off in the long term.

Worried about your toddler's limited diet?

If your child is growing in height and in weight (albeit maybe a little slowly), it is very likely that she is getting everything she needs. Letting your toddler continue to eat to their own appetite and make their own choices will stand them in good stead for their future health and relationship with food. With repeated exposure, plenty of choice and a calm attitude, it's likely that their fussiness will tail off, usually by age five. Of course, if you feel your child's restricted eating goes beyond typical childhood fussiness or that they are not receiving the nutrition that they need to grow, contact a health professional.

The juggle is real:

A guide to spinning plates and actually getting food on the table

I often find weaning advice misses out how to cook for your baby in practice. It's all very well knowing about the hows and whys of weaning, and having access to good recipes, but this isn't much help if you can't find the time to cook or clean up afterwards. I asked my followers on Instagram to share their biggest challenges when cooking and here are my solutions:

You need to cook dinner, but your baby just needs you!

Some of your cooking can be done while baby-wearing. If your baby's hands are safely tucked in, try chopping your ingredients with them in a **carrier**, minimising the amount of time they are out of your arms. I don't recommend cooking on the hob or taking things in and out of the oven with your baby attached to you though!

Prep as much as you can during your baby's nap or at a time when they are peacefully playing.

Slow-cooking can help, too. Switch on the slow cooker in the morning and serve up the food at dinner time.

Keep cooking simple. Quick-cook or slow-cooked is best, as are one-pot dishes that need only the odd one-handed stir.

Set timers as it is so easy to get distracted when you are trying to take care of a baby and cook at the same time (and usually on limited sleep!).

Your crawling/cruising baby roots through the cupboards, escapes the room and generally causes havoc while you try to cook.

Use novelty toys. Treasure baskets filled with sensory balls, scarves and instruments can be good, too, or even baskets filled with safe household items – babies love real things.

Give your baby some **safe ingredients** to handle. Butternut squashes make excellent drums and diced fresh herbs are wonderful to sniff.

Let them play with pots and pans. A classic!

If you have space, could you make your baby their **own little cupboard** filled with their cups, plates and Tupperware? Secure the other cupboards with safety locks.

If your baby does approach the oven, move them away quickly saying, **'Stop! Hot!'** You could invest in oven locks but the best thing you can do is to teach them right from the beginning that it is safer not to touch the oven at all.

Room dividers or playpens placed where you and your baby can see each other can work well to keep everyone safe.

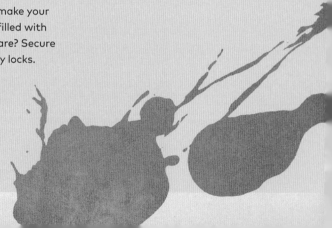

You are a working parent and find dinner time a real rush.

● Remember that lots of nutritious meals can be **cooked very quickly** and meals do not always need to be cooked completely from scratch.
● Try to **batch-cook** things like pesto pasta sauces if you can (but remember to pull meals out of the freezer on time).
● **Meal planning and online grocery** shopping will help to avoid the 'what do I cook' panic.

● **Cook just one meal for everyone.** Serving your baby pieces of food from a family meal, rather than puréeing or mashing, will cut out an extra step, too.
● **If you are breastfeeding**, expect your baby to potentially be more interested in milk than in food in the evenings.

You want your baby to learn how to feed herself but you just can't cope with the mess.

● Remember that **the mess is short-lived.** The more you let her do it, the better her control will be.
● **Spoon-feed** foods that really set you on edge (my husband has a real problem with loose rice).
● Avoid too much throwing by **putting less food in front of her**, so you can manage the clear up a little more easily. Provide lots of opportunities for throwing during the day if your baby likes to throw food.
● **Scoop bibs** are great for catching lumps; long sleeves are best for runnier foods.

● Try a shower curtain or **wipe-clean cloth under the highchair**. Scoop it all up and shake into the bin at the end of the meal.
● A follower once told me that the best way to clean up couscous was to hoover it up after it had dried. So, it isn't always best to clear up straight away!
● Have a stack of **reusable wipes** at the ready, though try not to clean up your baby until after the meal.
● I have lots of **non-crumbly snack recipes** that are ideal for confidently taking to restaurants. There are a few savoury muffin recipes that are perfect for this (see pages 182–185).

The Recipes

● ●

Before you start cooking...

My recipes are for days where you are too tired to think about meals. I have cooked and battle-tested them all with my three children and written off any that felt like extra work. The last thing I want to do is add to your to-do list.

The recipes have been designed with your baby's nutritional needs at the forefront as well as for family enjoyment. All are suitable from six months, once your baby has sampled a few tastes and experienced the allergens (see below). After you have tried a few recipes, you may feel confident enough to adapt your own cooking to make it baby friendly.

The recipes free from milk, soya, nuts, egg and gluten are marked with the symbols below, and you'll notice a snowflake symbol next to recipes that can be frozen. It's best to defrost in the fridge overnight. In terms of portions, the meals are based around a family of two adults and two to three babies or small children, unless stated otherwise. You should be able to easily scale up or down depending on how many you are feeding. Cooking times are based on a fan-assisted oven.

I wish you happy and minimal-stress cooking. Please remember that not all meals have to be perfectly balanced and it's fine to lean on convenience foods from time to time, too. You are doing your best.

● ●

Free-from 🥛 *milk*   ⋮ *soya*   *nuts*   *egg*   🌾 *gluten*

Can be frozen

breakfasts

Raspberry Baby Cereal

Commercial baby cereals can be so expensive! However, they are a nutritious and easy breakfast for busy mornings. This homemade option might save you a few pennies...

Makes
5–10 portions

Time
5 minutes

50g **instant oats**

40g **ground almonds**

1 **wheat biscuit**

2 tsp freeze-dried **raspberry powder**

Pour the oats and ground almonds into a mixing bowl.

Crumble in the wheat biscuit.

Sprinkle in the raspberry powder and mix gently.

To serve, simply add your choice of milk and mix. Alternatively, store in an airtight container for up to 1 month.

FREE FROM

Tip
You can buy the raspberry powder in some larger supermarkets, but if you can't get hold of any, you can simply add fresh raspberries right before serving.

Porridge Recipes

In my opinion, porridge is the perfect breakfast for babies! It's nutritious (oats are a great source of iron), quick to make and easy to eat. If your baby eats porridge a lot, it's worth finding ways to jazz up your oats for variety and exposure to different tastes and textures. Here are just a few ideas. Each recipe makes enough to feed two adults and two little ones, and takes around 10 minutes to cook.

ALL FREE FROM *(if gf oats and dairy-free milk are used)*

All recipes serve
2 adults
+ 2 little ones

Tip

You can sub the rolled oats in these recipes for fortified instant oats if you want to, just reduce the cooking time to 2 minutes and use a little less milk. I often use instant oats as they offer extra nutrition, however porridge oats, jumbo oats or rolled oats offer a chunkier texture. We mix and match for the best of both worlds!

Dreamy Pink Porridge

This yummy and pretty-looking porridge can be served straight away or cooked the night before and eaten cold, like overnight oats. My girls call it 'princess porridge'.

100g **rolled oats**
300ml **whole milk** or 'whole' oat milk
200ml **water**
150g **strawberries**, roughly diced

a few drops of **vanilla extract**
2 tbsp **full-fat Greek yoghurt** or dairy-free alternative

Add the oats, milk and water to a pan and place over a medium heat.

Bring to a simmer, then reduce the heat to low and add the strawberries and vanilla.

Cook for 8–10 minutes, stirring well to help break down the strawberries (this will colour your porridge).

Cook for a few more minutes until the oats are completely soft, then remove from the heat and stir through the Greek yoghurt (this has the added benefit of cooling down the hot porridge).

Allow to cool slightly before serving.

Pesto & Courgette Porridge

A toe in the water of savoury porridge! It's an odd concept for some, but really, it isn't too different to a risotto dish.

100g **rolled oats**
500ml **water**
50g **courgette**, grated
1 tbsp **pesto**
juice of ¼ **lemon**
1 tbsp **mascarpone**

Add the oats and water to a pan and bring to a simmer over a medium heat.

Add the grated courgette, reduce the heat to low and stir in the pesto.

Cook for about 8 minutes, then remove from the heat and stir in the lemon juice and mascarpone to finish.

Allow to cool slightly before serving.

Pear & Almond Porridge

Adding ground almonds to porridge, cereal and baking is an easy way to add nutrients and extra energy to meals. I always keep a packet in the cupboard.

100g **rolled oats**
100g ripe **pear**, finely diced or a pouch of pear purée
½ tsp **ground ginger**

400ml **whole milk** or almond milk, plus extra if needed
100ml **water**
50g **ground almonds**

Add the oats, pear, ginger, milk and water to a pan and place over a medium heat.

Bring to a simmer, then reduce the heat to low.

Cook for 8–10 minutes, stirring well and mashing the pear against the sides of the pan. Add a little more milk if needed.

Gently stir through the ground almonds.

Allow to cool slightly before serving.

Winter Spiced Porridge

A nice one for chilly winter starts, or even Christmas morning!

100g **rolled oats**
a handful of finely diced **dates**
1 tsp **mixed spice**, or to taste
400ml **whole milk** or 'whole' oat milk, plus extra if needed
100ml **water**
grated zest of 1 **orange**

Add the oats, dates, mixed spice, milk and water to a pan and place over a medium heat.

Bring to a simmer, then reduce the heat to low and add the orange zest.

Cook for 8–10 minutes, stirring well and adding a little more milk if needed, or more mixed spice if you wish.

Allow to cool slightly before serving.

Tip
You could serve with segments of the orange used for the zest in the recipe.

Mini Porridge Loaves ❄

This is one of my most popular baby breakfast recipes. These mini loaves are easy to hold and not too messy to eat. They double up as a handy toddler snack, too. There are lots of different ways you can make these, so I have provided the base recipe and a list of flavour combinations to choose from.

Makes
10–12 mini loaves
or muffins

Time
20 minutes

FOR THE BASE RECIPE
100g **porridge oats**
150ml **milk** (any)
100g **fruit purée** or mashed
  fruit (see list)
1 large **egg**
fruit for **topping** (see list)

Preheat the oven to 210°C (190°C fan) and lightly grease a 12-hole mini loaf tin (or a standard 900g/2lb loaf tin).

Mix the oats with the milk and your chosen fruit purée in a bowl. Whisk in the egg.

Spoon the mixture into the greased mini loaf tin and arrange your fruit on top.

Bake the mini loaves for 10–12 minutes (or a standard loaf tin for 20 minutes) until 'set'.

Allow to cool a little, then turn out from the mould or tin and serve, or cover and refrigerate for up to 24 hours.

FREE FROM *(if dairy-free milk and gf oats are used)*

Some flavour options:

100g fruit purée		Topped with...
Mashed banana	+	Blueberries
Pear purée/mashed pear with ginger	+	Blackberries
Apple and apricot purée	+	Sliced apricots
Peach purée	+	Raspberries
Coconut cream with cinnamon	+	Diced dates
Apple purée with vanilla	+	Strawberries

Freezing
Freeze the cooked loaves between sheets of greaseproof paper in a container or freezer bag for up to 3 months. Defrost in the fridge overnight. Warm over a low heat in the oven if required.

Pancakes

● ● ● ● ● ● ● ● ● ● ● ● ● ● ● ●

A good bank of pancake recipes is a must when you have a baby or toddler! They are ideal for babies who are new to solids, as they are easy to hold and soft to eat.

Tip

With pancakes, muffins and fritters, it's a good idea to serve the 'whole' version of key ingredients alongside. This will give your baby a range of tastes and textures, and will help them to link flavours with particular foods. For example, I would serve fresh banana sticks alongside the banana pancakes, and some of the smooth prune purée alongside the prune pancakes.

My First Banana Pancakes ❄

These are SO easy to make and an absolute winner in my house! Serve with fresh banana, squished blueberries and Greek yoghurt, and an optional squidge of maple syrup or honey for older children.

Makes
10 pancakes

Time
10 minutes

1 ripe **banana**
70ml **milk** (any)

70g **plain flour**
1 tbsp **sunflower oil**

Put the banana in a bowl and mash it well with a fork. Whisk in the milk and flour until you have a batter.

Heat the oil in a frying pan over a medium heat.

Working in batches, ladle in small amounts of the mixture and allow to cook for 1–2 minutes,

then flip with a spatula. Cook on the other side for 1–2 minutes until pale gold and slightly crispy (fritter-like) around the edges.

Remove from the frying pan and drain on kitchen paper before serving (to remove any excess oil).

FREE FROM *(if dairy-free milk is used)*

HONEY must not be served to babies under 12 months.

Spinach Smoothie Pancakes ❄

Green pancakes are really fun and a brilliant way of adding iron-rich greens into your baby's diet! In our house they have been known as 'spooky witch pancakes', 'dinosaur eggs' and even 'alien slime cakes'!

Makes
10–12 pancakes

Time
10 minutes

40g **spinach**
⅓ **mango**
½ **banana**
100ml **milk** (any, but coconut milk drink is quite nice)
100g **plain flour**
1 large **egg**
2 tbsp **sunflower oil**

Add the spinach, mango, banana and milk to a blender and blend until smooth.

Transfer to a bowl and whisk in the flour and the egg.

Heat the oil in a frying pan over a medium heat.

Working in batches, add tablespoonfuls of the mixture, quickly circling the back of the spoon on the mixture to form small circles of batter in the pan.

Cook for 2 minutes, then flip with a spatula. Press lightly with the back of the spatula and cook for another 2 minutes.

Slide the pancakes out of the pan. Both sides should be a mix of green and golden in colour.

FREE FROM *(if dairy-free milk is used)*

Prune Pouch Pancakes ❄

This pancake is a tasty way to include prunes at breakfast time (if you know, you know!). You can add a dash of cocoa for older ones for a chocolatey flavour, if you like. If prunes aren't your baby's thing, the recipe actually works really well with any fruit purée.

Makes
8 pancakes

Time:
10 minutes

100g **self-raising flour**
70g pouch **prune purée**
50ml **milk** (any)
1 large **egg**
1 tbsp **sunflower oil**

Whisk together the flour, purée, milk and egg in a bowl.

Heat the oil in a frying pan over a medium heat.

Working in batches, ladle small amounts into the pan and cook for 90 seconds–2 minutes, then flip with a spatula. Press lightly with the back of the spatula and cook for another minute, until the pancake is firm on the outside (the middle will be fluffy!).

FREE FROM *(if dairy-free milk is used)*

Fluffy American-style Pancakes

These are very versatile little pancakes. Potential toppings include banana and peanut butter, berry compote and yoghurt, salmon and cream cheese, avocado and soured cream... anything you like!

Makes:
8–10 pancakes

Time:
10 minutes

120g **self-raising flour**
⅓ tsp **baking powder**
2 **eggs**
120ml **milk** (any)
1 heaped tbsp **full-fat Greek yoghurt**
1 tbsp **sunflower oil**

Add the flour and baking powder to a mixing bowl.

Whisk together the eggs, milk and yoghurt in a separate bowl.

Tip the wet ingredients into the dry ingredients and whisk together.

Heat the oil in a frying pan over a medium heat and ladle in small amounts of the batter.

Cook until you see a few bubbles (this usually takes a couple of minutes), then flip and cook the other side for just a minute to finish.

Tip

If you prefer a thinner pancake, check out my crêpe recipe on page 168.

FREE FROM

Freezing

Place each pancake between a piece of greaseproof paper and freeze in an airtight container or freezer bag for up to 3 months. Defrost in the fridge overnight. Once defrosted, you can slightly warm them in a pan or in the oven on a low heat.

Storing pancakes

Store in an airtight container in the fridge for up to 24 hours.

Cheesy Courgette Pancakes

These are just the fluffiest savoury pancakes ever! Delicious served warm.

Makes
6–8

Time
10 minutes

100g **courgette** (about 1 small courgette), grated

2 **eggs**
60g **self-raising flour**
30g **Cheddar**, grated
2 tsp sunflower, rapeseed or olive **oil**

Squeeze out the extra liquid from the grated courgette using a clean tea towel or kitchen paper. Add to a large mixing bowl.

Whisk in the eggs, then add the flour and grated Cheddar. Mix well.

Heat the oil in a frying pan and ladle in small amounts of the batter.

Cook for 1 minute, then flip over and cook the other side for 1 minute until golden and slightly crispy.

FREE FROM

Tomato Pancakes

We love these warm, topped with melty butter! You could go one step further and serve with finely diced basil and fresh mozzarella.

Makes
10–12 pancakes

Time
10 minutes

2 **eggs**
150g **tinned chopped tomatoes**
150g **self-raising flour**
1 tbsp **cream cheese**
1 tsp **dried oregano**
1 tbsp **sunflower oil**

In a large mixing bowl, whisk the eggs, tomatoes and flour together. Mix in the cream cheese and oregano.

Heat the oil in a frying pan over a medium heat and, working in batches, ladle in small amounts of the batter.

Cook until bubbles appear on the top, then flip them over and cook the other side for around 1 minute until crisp.

FREE FROM

Tahini Toast

Tahini is high in calcium, iron, B vitamins and zinc. It's also a great alternative to peanut butter for babies who have, or may have, a peanut allergy. Tahini has a stronger taste than peanut butter and is a little thick on its own, so I mix it with banana to make a delicious spread.

● ●

Serves
1 adult
+ 1 little one

Time
2 minutes

2 slices of **bread**
½ **banana**
2 tsp **tahini**
a pinch of **ground cinnamon**

● ●

Toast the bread.

Mash the banana in a bowl, then mix in the tahini and cinnamon until the spread looks slightly glossy. Spread over the toast.

Cut into strips or squares for baby and serve.

● ●

FREE FROM *(if soya-free bread is used)*

Tip
For toddlers, adding a little bit of cocoa powder turns this into a pretty convincing chocolate spread...

Apricot & Almond Breakfast Balls

This breakfast is very quick to prep and can be done the night before to speed things up on busy mornings. These are perfect for beginners and don't make too much mess.

Makes
4

Time
5 minutes

1 **wheat biscuit**
40ml **milk** (any)
2 dried **apricots**,
   finely diced
3 tbsp **ground almonds**

Mash the wheat biscuit in a bowl. Add the milk, apricots and 2 tablespoons of the ground almonds.

Divide the mixture into four even pieces and roll them into balls.

Roll through the remaining 1 tablespoon almonds to coat.

Serve straight away or cover and refrigerate for up to 2 days.

FREE FROM *(if dairy-free milk is used)*

Variations

You can play around with the flavours here, using dates or sultanas instead of apricot, trying different milks or adding a sprinkle of ginger or cinnamon.

Cashew & Blueberry Pinwheels ❄

Nut butters are a great source of energy, fat and protein for babies. I love the flavour and texture combination of creamy cashew and juicy blueberry... I hope your baby does, too!

● ●

Makes:
6–8

Time:
25 minutes
(30 minutes chilling)

200g **banana**
    (about 2 small bananas)
2 heaped tbsp **cashew butter**
320g **ready-rolled puff pastry**
100g **blueberries**
sunflower oil spray

● ●

Preheat the oven to 200°C (180°C fan) and line a baking tray with greaseproof paper.

Mash the banana in a bowl. Add the cashew butter, mixing it in well.

Take the pastry sheet straight from the fridge (it needs to be cold). Carefully unroll it and quickly spread over the banana and cashew butter mixture (you need to work quickly so the pastry doesn't go soggy). Drop the blueberries on top of the banana and cashew layer. Roll up tightly and refrigerate for at least 30 minutes.

After chilling, slice the roll into 6–8 wheels by pointing a sharp knife into the pastry and slicing down carefully. Place the wheels flat on the lined baking tray and spray with sunflower oil (alternatively you could brush with milk or egg). Bake for 20 minutes.

Allow to cool, then serve, or store in an airtight container for 24 hours.

● ●

FREE FROM

❄ **Freezing**
Freeze raw, prior to baking, for up to 3 months. To cook from frozen, bake for 25 minutes at 210°C (190°C fan).

Apple & Pear Traybake

Raw apples are a no-no for babies, as they pose a choking hazard. It's best to soften them by cooking. Ripe pears are fine to serve raw, but, like apples, need softening if they are hard. This recipe is perfectly soft and really nutritious! Just add yoghurt for a complete breakfast.

Serves
1 adult
+ 1 little one

Time
25 minutes

2 **apples**, cored and sliced (you can peel for younger babies, if you like)
2 **pears**, cored and sliced (you can peel for younger babies, if you like)
2 tbsp **nut butter**
½ tsp **ground cinnamon**
50ml **milk** (any)
a handful of **porridge oats**

Preheat the oven to 210°C (190°C fan).

Place the sliced fruit on a baking tray or dish.

Mix together the nut butter, cinnamon and milk in a bowl, then pour onto the fruit. Sprinkle over the oats and toss together by hand.

Bake in the preheated oven for 15–20 minutes; the fruit should be soft enough to squish, but not falling apart. Serve immediately.

FREE FROM *(if dairy-free milk and gf oats are used)*

Cheesy Stove-top Oatcakes

These are a cross between a cheese oatcake and a porridge pancake. They are perfect for babies who are just starting solids, as they are very soft and 'grab-able'! Try them with ripe pear slices for a sweet/savoury breakfast.

● ●

Makes
8–10

Time
5 minutes

● ● ● ● ● ● ● ● ● ●

80g **rolled oats**
100ml **milk** (any)
40g **cheddar**, grated
1 tbsp **sunflower oil**

Mix the oats, milk and cheese in a bowl.

Heat the oil in a frying pan over a medium heat.

Spoon in level tablespoons of the oat mixture (don't worry, it looks like it won't stick together, but I promise it will!) and cook for 2 minutes, shaping each oatcake gently into a circle with a spatula.

Flip the oatcakes (if they look like they might break apart, leave them to cook for a few more seconds before flipping), then press down with the spatula and cook for another 2 minutes until golden.

Serve immediately.

● ●

FREE FROM *(if gf oats and soya-free milk are used)*

Mexican Hash Brown Bites

This is a proper weekend breakfast for the whole family. Serve with guacamole or soured cream and an extra squeeze of lime.

● ●

Makes
12

Time
15 minutes

● ● ● ● ● ● ● ● ● ● ● ●

100g **potato** (about
 ½ large potato),
 grated
100g **sweet potato**
 (about ½ large sweet
 potato), grated
⅓ **onion**, grated
80g **broccoli**, grated
 (leave the bottom of
 the stem)
2 tsp **smoked paprika**
½ tsp **garlic powder**
30g **Cheddar**, grated
1–2 tbsp fresh **coriander**,
 to taste
juice of 1 **lime**
2 **eggs**

● ●

FREE FROM

Preheat the oven to 220°C (200°C fan). Grease a 12-hole cupcake tin really well (to avoid sticking).

Squeeze out the extra liquid from the grated potato and sweet potato using a clean tea towel or kitchen paper. Add to a large mixing bowl.

Add the grated onion and broccoli, paprika, garlic powder and grated cheese to the mixture. Tear in the coriander, squeeze in the lime juice and whisk in the eggs.

Divide the mixture between the 12 greased holes of the cupcake tin and press down lightly.

Bake in the preheated oven for 10 minutes.

Use a spoon to remove each 'bite' and serve immediately.

Freezing

Pop the bites in a freezer bag or container, separated by greaseproof paper if you can, and freeze for up to 3 months. To reheat, bake in the oven for 15 minutes at 220°C (200°C fan).

Variation

You can also cook these 'fritter-style' in a frying pan with a little olive oil for 3 minutes on each side.

Tip

Try this with my homemade Speedy Ketchup (see page 137) – delicious!

Avocado Eggy Bread

This is a staple in our house, and a great one for a family breakfast or brunch at the weekend.

● ●

Serves
2 adults
+ 1–2 little ones

Time
10 minutes

2 ripe **avocados**
2 large **eggs**
1 tbsp **olive oil**
4 slices of **bread**
a small handful of grated **Cheddar** (optional, and not too much for baby!)

● ●

Mash the avocados in a bowl with a fork, then whisk in the eggs.

Heat the oil in a frying pan over a medium heat.

Dip a slice of bread in the egg mixture, then place it straight in the hot pan and sprinkle with a little cheese, if using.

Cook for 2 minutes, then flip and cook on the other side for 90 seconds–2 minutes until greeny-golden in colour.

Repeat with the remaining slices of bread.

Serve immediately.

● ●

FREE FROM *(if cheese is omitted and soya-free bread is used)*

Mushroom & Cress Omelette

Omelettes make excellent finger food for babies.
I find that thicker omelettes are best, as you can
cut them into chunky wedges, which are ideal for
little hands to grasp.

Serves:
1 adult
+ 1 baby

Time:
10 minutes

2 **eggs**
50g **mushrooms**, grated
1–2 handfuls of **cress**
   or other microgreens
15g **Cheddar**, grated
   (optional)
1 tbsp sunflower, rapeseed
   or olive **oil**

Lightly whisk the eggs, then add the grated
mushrooms. Sprinkle in the cress and the grated
cheese. Mix well.

Heat the oil in a small frying pan over a medium
heat. Once hot, pour in the mixture, swirling the pan
for even coverage.

Let the omelette cook for around 90 seconds before
flipping one half of the omelette onto the other,
pressing gently with a spatula (this creates a big
fluffy omelette, perfect for slicing).

Cook the folded omelette for another minute on
each side, then slide it out of the pan, cut into
wedges and serve immediately.

FREE FROM *(if cheese is omitted)*

Variations

Try grating
in courgette,
tearing in
spinach or
adding a few
diced spring
onions.

Smokey Beans

This recipe is delicious at any time of day really, but it makes a brilliant savoury breakfast served with toast and avocado. It's a pretty convincing alternative to tinned beans!

● ●

Serves:
2 adults
+ 2–3 little ones

Time:
30 minutes

● ● ● ● ● ● ● ● ● ● ● ●

400g **tinned haricot beans,** or cannellini

400g **tinned chopped tomatoes**

1 tsp **garlic purée**

2 tsp **smoked paprika**

100ml **apple juice**

1 tsp **dried oregano**

1 tsp **olive oil**

Add the beans and chopped tomatoes to a pan and place over a high heat. Add all the other ingredients except the olive oil, gently stirring them in.

Cook over a high heat for 5 minutes until simmering, then turn down and cook over a low heat for 20 minutes, stirring occasionally, until the sauce is thick and slightly sticky and the beans are nicely softened.

Stir through the olive oil for a silky finish.

Serve immediately, or cover and refrigerate for up to 2 days.

● ●

FREE FROM

Variation

You can speed this up by making a microwave version. Just pop all the ingredients in a bowl, cover and microwave for 4 minutes, stirring halfway through.

Freezing

Freeze in an airtight container for up to 3 months.

Spanish-style Breakfast Tray Bake

This cooked breakfast is brilliant for pincer grip practise for babies aged around eight months and up. This isn't just a dish for breakfast of course – it makes a tasty supper dish, too.

Serves
2 adults
+ 2 little ones

Time
35 minutes

2 large **baking potatoes**, cut into 2cm cubes
2 tsp **dried oregano**
1 tsp **dried rosemary**
2 tsp **smoked paprika**
1 tsp **garlic powder**
2 tbsp **olive oil**
150g **cherry tomatoes**, quartered
4–6 **eggs**
3 handfuls of **kale**
juice of ½ **lemon**
black pepper

Tip
Toddlers and older children may enjoy this with some smokey chorizo, too. Just finely dice and sprinkle it over before it goes in the oven.

Preheat the oven to 210°C (190°C fan).

In a mixing bowl, toss the potatoes with the herbs, paprika, garlic powder and 1 tablespoon of the olive oil.

Spread the seasoned potatoes over a baking dish and bake in the preheated oven for 15 minutes.

Add the cherry tomatoes to the tray, toss everything together and bake for a further 20 minutes until the potatoes are soft.

Meanwhile, bring a pan of water to the boil and add the eggs. Cook for 8 minutes, then transfer to a bowl of cold water (to stop them from cooking any further).

When the potatoes and tomatoes are cooked, tear in the kale and drizzle over the remaining 1 tablespoon of olive oil.

Return to the oven for a few minutes, just until the kale is crisp (take care not to burn it), then remove the tray from the oven, squeeze over the lemon juice and sprinkle over some black pepper.

Peel and quarter the boiled eggs and arrange them on top of the vegetables before bringing to the table.

FREE FROM

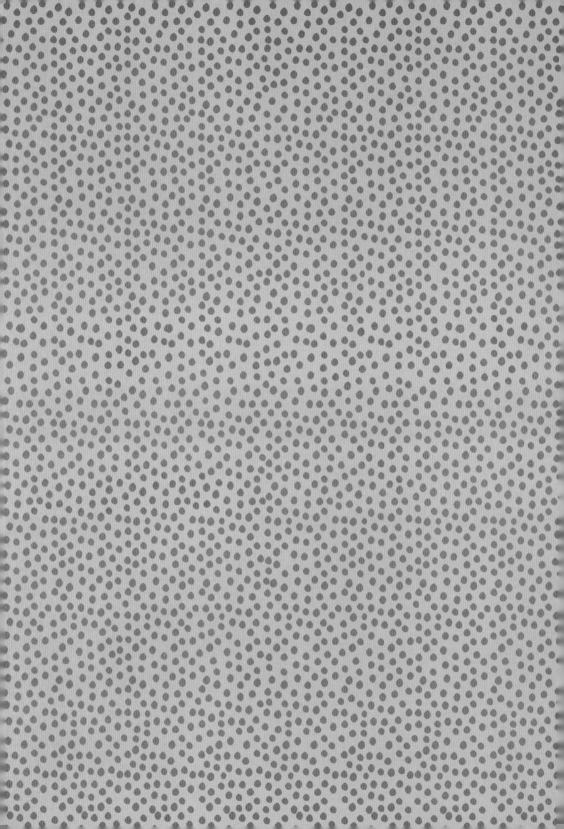

lunches & light bites

Chicken Salad

Salad is for babies, too! Big leafy affairs covered in dressing –
probably not... but pieces of cold veg, a source of protein and a
baby-safe dressing are a big yes! Here's one idea. I have left the
quantities off the recipe, so you can just add what you have to hand.

Time
15 minutes

Tenderstem broccoli
large **vine tomatoes**
cucumber
ripe **avocado**
cold cooked **chicken**
   (leftovers work
   well here)
soured cream
lemon juice
olive oil
black pepper

Cook the Tenderstem broccoli in a pan of
boiling water for 5–6 minutes (or steam
for 3–4 minutes) until soft enough for
your baby to eat.

Slice the tomatoes, cucumber and
avocado into long pieces or wedges
(or smaller pieces if your baby uses a
pincer grip).

Tear the chicken into strips (or small
pieces if your baby can manage).

To make the dressing, mix a tablespoon
of soured cream with a squeeze of
lemon juice, a glug of olive oil and a
sprinkle of black pepper in a bowl.

Toss the ingredients and the dressing
together in a bowl.

To serve, lay one of each ingredient on
your baby's tray or plate. That way they
can see what's on offer!

FREE FROM

Variation

Try swapping the chicken
for salmon or strips of very
thin steak.

Baby Prawn Salad

UK advice is that it's absolutely fine for babies to eat well cooked seafood. Just treat it as an allergen and introduce separately to other common allergens. This recipe can be enjoyed either on its own (perhaps with some cooked couscous mixed in) or as a filling for wraps or sandwiches once your baby is a bit older.

Serves
1 adult
+ 1 little one

Time
5 minutes

1 ripe **avocado**
100g cooked **prawns**, finely diced
1 tbsp **soured cream** or dairy-free crème fraîche alternative
juice of ½ **lemon**
a pinch of **paprika**
black pepper

Mash the avocado in a large bowl using a fork.

Add the cooked prawns, soured cream, lemon juice, paprika and a little black pepper.

Give everything a stir and serve immediately.

FREE FROM *(if dairy-free alternative is used)*

Tuna & Chickpea Salad

This is a family recipe that we have always enjoyed in the summer. For babies, lightly squash the chickpeas and let them scoop the mixture up with their hands. You could stir in some cooked couscous or serve with green beans.

Serves
2 adults
+ 2 little ones

Time
5 minutes

180g **tinned tuna** in spring water, drained
240g **tinned chickpeas** or flageolet beans, drained
2 large **vine tomatoes**, finely diced
a handful of **fresh parsley**, finely diced or 1 tsp dried
1 tbsp **olive oil**
juice of ½ **lemon**
black pepper

FREE FROM

Put the tuna, chickpeas, tomatoes and parsley in a large bowl.

Add the olive oil, lemon juice and a pinch of black pepper, then gently mix together.

Serve in little bowls, mashed for your baby, if you prefer.

Tip

When shopping for tuna, check the sodium levels on the side of the tin. Different brands vary in terms of salt content – always pick the lowest.

Giant Couscous Salad

This colourful salad is surprisingly easy to grab, making it ideal for self-feeding babies. Just add your protein of choice to turn it into a complete meal. Boiled eggs work well!

Serves
1 adult
+ 1–2 little ones

Time
5 minutes

50g **giant couscous**

100g **butternut squash**,
   peeled and roughly diced

70g **broccolini** or broccoli,
   cut into small spears

50g **mango**, cut into
   1.5cm cubes

2 tbsp finely diced
   fresh parsley

1 tbsp **olive oil**

juice of ½ **lemon**

Bring a pan of water to the boil and add the couscous, butternut squash and broccolini. Cook for 10 minutes or until the couscous is soft. Drain the excess water.

Add the mango, parsley, olive oil and lemon juice.

Serve warm or cold, or cover and store in the fridge for up to 2 days.

FREE FROM

Greek-style Courgette Fritters

I love the combination of mint, garlic, fresh courgette and sharp feta in this recipe. These are best served warm with a tomato dip or my minty Tzatziki (see page 137).

Makes
6–8

Time
10 minutes

- 100g **courgette** (about 1 small courgette), grated
- 100g **fine semolina**
- ½ tsp **garlic powder**
- ½ tsp **dried mint**
- 2 **eggs**
- 40g **feta cheese**, crumbled
- 1 tbsp **olive oil**

Squeeze out the extra liquid from the grated courgette using a clean tea towel or kitchen paper. Add to a large mixing bowl.

Add the semolina, garlic powder and mint, and mix.

Whisk in the eggs, then sprinkle in the cheese and mix gently.

Heat the oil in a frying pan over a medium heat.

Once hot, add spoonfuls of the batter and cook the fritters for 3 minutes on each side, flipping twice during cooking, until they are golden.

Remove from the frying pan and drain on kitchen to remove any excess oil.

Serve straight away.

FREE FROM

Variation

Instead of feta and mint, you could try Cheddar and chives.

Frittata Nests

I love serving eggs like this. All the goodness of eggs, plus fresh little bites of pea, tomato, mint and feta. Just make sure you leave some for your baby!

● ●

Makes
10–12

Time
20 minutes

● ● ● ● ● ● ● ●

5 **eggs**

50g **peas** (fresh or frozen, defrosted)

1 **salad tomato**, finely diced (you can leave the seeds in)

2 tsp **dried mint**

40g **feta cheese**, crumbled

Preheat the oven to 220°C (200°C fan). Lightly grease a 12-hole muffin tin (I spray with oil).

Whisk the eggs in a bowl. Add the peas, tomato and mint to the egg mixture, then crumble in the feta and gently mix everything together.

Divide the frittata mixture among the 12 holes of the muffin tin and bake in the preheated oven for 12–15 minutes, or until the tops of the nests are visibly 'set'.

Serve straight away.

● ●

FREE FROM

Crispy Broccoli Fritters

My little ones love these with tomato sauce (homemade for baby, see my recipe on page 137) or a lemony yoghurt dip. They are about as quick to make as a sandwich!

Makes
6–8

Time
5 minutes

80g **cooked broccoli**
1 **egg**
100g **fine polenta**
70ml **milk**
1–2 handfuls of grated
   Cheddar
a pinch of **garlic powder**
1 tbsp **sunflower oil**
black pepper

Mash the broccoli in a large bowl using a fork. Whisk in the egg, then add the polenta, milk, grated cheese, garlic powder and a pinch of black pepper. Mix well.

Heat the oil in a frying pan over a medium heat.

Once hot, dollop in spoonfuls of the fritter batter and fry gently for 2 minutes on each side, or until golden and crisp all over.

Place on kitchen paper to remove any excess oil, then serve straight away.

FREE FROM

Mashed Potato Bites

•••••••••••••••••••••••••••••••••••••

Mashed potato bites are really useful if your baby is just starting to feed herself. They are also great if YOU are feeling anxious about offering pieces of food as they are so soft. Try offering your baby one of these recipes alongside some cooked vegetables.

•••••••••••••••••••••••••••••••

FREE FROM *(if dairy-free alternatives are used and Cheddar omitted)*

All recipes make
10–12 bites

Time
25 minutes

Chicken Pie Bites ❄

•••

150g **potato** (about 1 medium potato), peeled and roughly diced or leftover mash

about 40g leftover **roast chicken**, shredded

1–2 **mushrooms**, finely diced

1 tbsp **cream cheese** or dairy-free alternative

½ tsp **dried parsley** or tarragon

¼ tsp **garlic powder**

olive oil spray

Preheat the oven to 210°C (190°C fan). Lightly grease a baking tray or mini muffin tin with the olive oil spray.

Bring a pan of water to the boil, add the potato and cook for about 15 minutes until soft.

Drain, then transfer to a large bowl and add the chicken, diced mushrooms, cream cheese, herbs and garlic powder. Mash everything together.

Roll into tablespoon sized balls and place on the lightly greased baking tray or in the holes of the mini muffin tin. Spritz with the olive oil spray (this will help them to crisp up).

Bake in the preheated oven for 15 minutes until the bites are crisp on the outside. Cool slightly before serving.

 Freezing

Freeze prior to cooking. Spoon the potato bites onto a lined baking tray and freeze until solid, then transfer to a freezer bag or container and freeze for up to 3 months. Cook from frozen for 20 minutes at 220°C (200°C fan), until piping hot all the way through.

Bubble & Squeak Bites ❄

100g leftover **cooked veg** (carrots, parsnips, broccoli, peas...)

100g leftover **mashed potato**

a small handful of grated **mature Cheddar** or dairy-free alternative

Preheat the oven to 210°C (190°C fan). Lightly grease a mini muffin tin.

Mix the vegetables and the mashed potato in a mixing bowl.

Spoon the mixture into the mini muffin tin and top with the grated cheese.

Bake in the preheated oven for 20 minutes until crispy on top.

Use a tablespoon to remove (they should curl into balls as you do so) and leave to cool slightly before serving.

Salmon & Butternut Bites ❄

100g **potato** (about ½ large potato), peeled and roughly diced

80g **butternut squash**, peeled and roughly diced

60g skinless and boneless **tinned salmon** or leftover cooked salmon fillet

1 tsp **single cream** or dairy-free alternative

1 tsp **paprika**

1 tsp **dried parsley**

a small handful of grated **Cheddar** (optional)

Preheat the oven to 210°C (190°C fan). Lightly grease a baking tray or mini muffin tin.

Add the potato to a large pan, cover with boiling water and bring to the boil. Boil for 5 minutes, then add the squash.

Boil for another 10 minutes, or until soft, then drain and mash.

Transfer the mashed potato and squash to a large bowl and add the salmon, cream, paprika and parsley.

Roll into tablespoon-sized balls and place on the lightly greased baking tray or in the holes of the mini muffin tin. Sprinkle over the grated cheese.

Bake in the preheated oven for 15 minutes until the bites are crisp on the outside. Cool slightly before serving.

Tip
You can cook the potato and squash ahead of time if easier.

Pesto & Red Pepper Pinwheels

These are quick to make and always look impressive. They can be enjoyed both warm from the oven and cool.

Makes
8

Time
30 mins
(+ 30 mins chilling)

200g ready-rolled **puff pastry**

3 tbsp **green pesto** (see page 140 for my pesto recipes)

¼ head of **broccoli**, grated (leave the bottom of the stem)

½ **red pepper**, finely diced

a small handful of grated **Cheddar**

milk (any), for brushing

Unroll the pastry and spread over the pesto.

Sprinkle over the grated broccoli, diced red pepper and the grated cheddar (go easy for little ones).

Roll up tightly, cover and refrigerate for 30 minutes.

Meanwhile, preheat the oven to 210°C (190°C fan) and line a baking sheet with greaseproof paper.

Remove the rolled-up pastry from the fridge and slice into eight rounds with a sharp knife (I find it helps to point the knife straight down into the pastry to avoid it getting squashed).

Place each pinwheel flat on the baking sheet, spaced out evenly, and brush with a small amount of milk.

Bake in the centre of the preheated oven for 15–20 minutes, until the pastry is crisp and golden. Allow to cool, then serve, or store in an airtight container for up to 24 hours.

FREE FROM

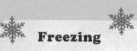

❄ Freezing ❄

Freeze raw, prior to baking, for up to 3 months. To cook from frozen, bake for 25 minutes at 210°C (190°C fan).

Cheese & Tomato Pizza Bites

These tomatoey little bites are kind of a cross between falafel, arancini and... pizza?! They taste brilliant served warm with a soured cream dip. You can also eat them cold.

● ●

Makes
10–12

Time
30 minutes

● ● ● ● ● ● ● ● ● ● ●

50g **rice** (brown or white)
100g **chickpeas**
6 **cherry tomatoes,**
   finely diced
a few leaves of **spinach**,
   finely torn (optional)
1 tsp **dried oregano**
1 tsp **paprika** (optional)
30–40g **Cheddar**, grated

Preheat the oven to 220°C (200°C fan) and line a baking tray with greaseproof paper.

Cook the rice according to the packet instructions.

Add the chickpeas, tomatoes, spinach, oregano and paprika to a mixing bowl.

Once cooked, add the rice to the bowl, then add the cheese.

Pulse the mixture with a hand blender (or mash well with a potato masher).

Scoop tablespoon-sized amounts onto the lined baking tray and bake in the preheated oven for 20 minutes until the outside is crisp and the middle is soft and slightly gooey. Leave to cool slightly before serving.

● ●

FREE FROM

Tip
Take care when cooking and reheating rice. If you can, make the bites immediately after cooking the rice. If you do use leftover rice, make sure it is cooled quickly after cooking, stored in the fridge for no more than 24 hours and cooked until piping hot (these will be!).

Florentine Pizza Pitta

A crowd-pleasing lunch that can be adapted in lots of different ways. Try making this baby-friendly recipe on family pizza nights, so even the littlest family members can join in the fun! Recipe makes one pizza pitta, so scale up if you want to make them for the whole family.

● ●

Makes
1

Time
20 mins, plus chilling

● ● ● ● ● ● ● ● ● ● ●

1 **pitta**
1 tbsp **tomato purée**
½ tsp **dried oregano**
¼ tsp **garlic powder**
½ tsp **olive oil**
a few **spinach leaves**,
   torn into small pieces
1 **mushroom**, grated
   or finely diced
1 **egg**
sprinkle of grated
   Italian hard cheese
   (more for grown-ups!)

Preheat the oven to 220°C (200°C fan) and lightly grease a baking tray.

Place the pitta on the lightly greased baking tray.

Mix the tomato purée, oregano, garlic powder and olive oil in a small bowl, the spread the tomato sauce over the pitta.

Top with the spinach and mushroom, then very carefully crack the egg on top.

Sprinkle over a little Italian hard cheese and bake in the preheated oven for 10–12 minutes until the white of the egg is completely cooked.

● ●

FREE FROM

Variations

You can add any leftover veg, grated courgette or fresh tomato slices. If your little one can't have egg, you could add mozzarella, leftover cooked meats or tinned fish.

Baby Spanakopita ❄

Spanakopita is a Greek pastry filled with spinach and feta. It is usually made with crispy filo pastry, which can be a little bit too spikey for babies, so I have used puff pastry instead. I have also used just enough feta to provide the 'tang' without the recipe becoming salty.

Makes
8

Time
20 minutes

50g **spinach**

30g **feta cheese**
(you can add a little more for children over 12 months)

1 tsp **dried mint**

150g **ready-rolled puff pastry**

1 tsp **olive oil**

Preheat the oven to 220°C (200°C fan). Line a baking tray with greaseproof paper.

Blend the spinach, feta and mint in a blender, or with a hand blender.

Slice the pastry sheet into four long rectangles and spread the green filling evenly over the pastry.

Fold each rectangle in half, then slice again to make two smaller rectangles.

Seal the edges by pressing lightly with a fork.

Place on the lined baking tray and brush over the olive oil.

Bake in the preheated oven for about 12 minutes until the pastry is golden.

Leave to cool slightly before serving warm, or allow to cool and store in an airtight container in the fridge for up to 2 days.

FREE FROM *(if egg-free puff pastry used)*

❄ Freezing

Freeze prior to cooking. To cook from frozen, bake for 20 minutes at 220°C (200°C fan).

Simple Fishcakes ❄

These very simple fishcakes make a delicious warm lunch or light dinner. Add some greens on the side and serve with a poached egg on top to complete the meal.

Makes
10–12

Time
6 minutes

200g **potato** (about 1 large potato), peeled and diced

100g **tinned tuna** in spring water, drained well

1 **spring onion**, finely diced

1 tsp **dried parsley**

1 **egg**

70g **breadcrumbs**

1 tbsp **sunflower oil**

Bring a pan of water to the boil, add the potato and cook for about 15 minutes until soft but not completely mushy. Drain and then return to the hot pan (this will help any excess water to evaporate).

Add the tuna, spring onion and parsley to the potato, and mash everything together using a potato masher.

Whisk the egg in a small bowl and sprinkle the breadcrumbs onto a large plate.

Tear off a tablespoon-sized amount of the tuna and potato mixture and roll into a ball.

Dip the ball briefly into the egg and then roll in the breadcrumbs. Place on a plate. Repeat until you have used all the mixture

Heat the oil in a frying pan over a medium heat. When the oil is hot, place the fishcakes into the oil and gently flatten with a spatula. Cook for around 3 minutes on each side, or until crisp.

FREE FROM 🥛 ⬛ *(if soya-free breadcrumbs used)*

Variation

If you get side-tracked before the cooking stage (e.g. if baby wakes up early from their nap!), just roll the tuna, cooked potato and parsley into balls for your baby to pick up and eat. Still yummy! Alternatively, you can also bake the fishcakes for 15 minutes at 220°C (200°C fan).

Freezing

Freeze on a lined baking tray until solid, then transfer to a freezer bag or container and freeze for up to 3 months. To reheat, defrost in the fridge overnight, then bake for 15 minutes at 220°C (200°C fan).

Turkey Goujons ❄

This is my homemade take on the classic nugget – ideal for toddlers who are going through a 'beige stage'!

Makes
12

Time
25 minutes

300g **turkey mince**
1 tbsp **dried mixed herbs**
1 tsp **garlic powder**
1 **egg**
60g **breadcrumbs**
sunflower oil spray

Preheat the oven to 210°C (190°C fan). Lightly grease a baking tray.

Combine the turkey mince with the herbs and garlic powder by hand.

Whisk the egg in a bowl. Tip the breadcrumbs into another bowl.

Tear off tablespoon-sized pieces of the turkey mince mixture, and dip first into the egg and then coat with the breadcrumbs. Place on the lightly greased baking tray.

Lightly spray with oil (this will give a golden finish) and bake in the preheated oven for exactly 20 minutes.

FREE FROM   *(if soya-free breadcrumbs used)*

Variation
These also work well with pork mince.

Freezing
Place the cooked and cooled goujons on a lined baking tray and freeze until solid, then transfer to a freezer bag or container and freeze for up to 3 months. To reheat, defrost in the fridge overnight, then cook for 20 minutes at 220°C (200°C fan), until piping hot all the way through.

Carrot, Sweet Potato & Coconut Soup

Your baby will love exploring the exciting Thai-inspired flavours in this smooth soup! You can serve it thick or thin it out with extra water if you prefer.

Serves
2 adults
+ 2–3 little ones

Time
40 minutes

1 tbsp **olive oil**

1 **onion**, diced

250g **sweet potato**
(about 2 sweet potatoes),
roughly diced

200g **carrot** (about 2 carrots),
roughly diced

300ml **low-salt**
vegetable stock,
plus extra if needed

400ml **tinned coconut milk**

1 tsp **ginger purée**

1 tsp **lemongrass purée**
or dried lemongrass

1 tsp **garlic purée**
or 1 clove of garlic

a small handful
of **fresh coriander**

Heat the oil in a large saucepan over a medium heat, add the onion and cook until it begins to soften.

Add the sweet potato, carrot, stock, coconut milk, ginger, lemongrass and garlic, and stir.

Once bubbling, turn down the heat to low, cover with a lid and simmer for 30 minutes, or until the vegetables are soft. Add a little more liquid if needed.

Blend the soup with a hand blender until smooth, then tear in the fresh coriander. Serve immediately, or allow to cool and refrigerate in an airtight container for up to 2 days.

FREE FROM *(if gf stock is used)*

Freezing ❄️
Freeze for up to 3 months. To reheat, defrost fully and cook on the hob or in the microwave until piping hot.

Serving tip

This is a good one for older babies to practise their spoon skills, or you can soak bread in the soup and bake for 10 minutes for an easy-to-grip option!

Classic Roast Chicken Soup

Use up leftover roast chicken and odds and ends of veg in this cosy soup. This is a lovely recipe to serve when everyone is feeling a bit run down, or when your baby is teething and wanting something soft.

Serves
2 adults
+ 2–3 little ones

Time
40 minutes

1 tbsp **olive oil**

1 large **onion**, diced

3 **carrots**, peeled and diced

2 **parsnips**, peeled and diced

1 **potato**, peeled and cut into 2cm cubes

1 tsp **dried parsley**

½ tsp **dried thyme**

½ tsp **dried rosemary**

400ml **low-salt chicken stock**, plus extra if needed

150g **frozen peas**

about 350g leftover **roast chicken**, shredded

1 tbsp **full-fat crème fraîche** or dairy-free alternative

a squeeze of **lemon juice**

black pepper

Heat the oil in a large saucepan over a medium heat, add the onion and cook until it begins to soften. Add the carrots, parsnips, potato and the herbs, and cook for a few minutes.

Add the stock and the frozen peas, and bring to the boil, then turn the heat down to low and simmer for 15 minutes.

Add the shredded chicken, gently stir, then cover with a lid and cook for a further 10–15 minutes until the vegetables are soft. Add more low-salt stock or water if needed.

Turn off the heat and gently stir through the crème fraîche, lemon juice and a pinch of black pepper. Serve immediately.

FREE FROM

(if dairy-free milk and gf stock is used)

Serving tip

For under 12-month-olds, you can pull out the chicken and veg and let baby pick them up, then soak a little bit of bread in the liquid. You can also blend the soup if your baby prefers smoother textures.

One-pan Cheese & Tomato Orzo

This is my go to 'kids only' dinner if my partner and I are choosing to eat later. It's very easy to eat and the flavours are comforting and familiar. There's a fair amount of veg in this dish, too! The recipe makes enough for a family of four for lunch, so just adjust the quantities if you need more/less.

● ●

Serves
2 adults
+ 2–3 little ones

Time
20 minutes

● ● ● ● ● ● ● ● ● ● ●

300g **orzo**
400g **tinned chopped tomatoes**
1 small **carrot**, grated
½ **courgette**, grated
3 florets **broccoli**, grated
3 **mushrooms**, grated
80g **frozen peas**
1 tbsp **dried oregano**
1 tbsp **smoked paprika**
1 tbsp **garlic powder**
a squeeze of **lemon**
a spoonful of **mascarpone**
a handful of grated **Cheddar**

Add the orzo to a large pan, cover with boiling water and cook over a medium heat for 3 minutes.

Add the chopped tomatoes, carrot, courgette, broccoli, mushrooms, peas, oregano, paprika and garlic powder. Mix everything together.

Reduce the heat to low and put a lid on the pan. Cook for 10 minutes, stirring regularly to avoid sticking, until the orzo is soft,

Remove from the heat and leave to cool for a minute, then add a squeeze of lemon juice, the mascarpone and the grated Cheddar.

Gently stir together and check for temperature (it gets very hot!) before serving.

● ●

FREE FROM

Super-quick Salmon & Pea Pasta

I have included this in the lunch section because it is so speedy, but of course you could serve it for dinner, too. I try to always have the ingredients for this in the house – it's my 'zombie apocalypse' meal! Perfect for getting home late, cooking with a clingy baby, date nights... basically any situation!

Serves
2 adults
+ 2–3 little ones

Time
10 minutes

300g **fresh pasta**
150g **frozen peas**
1 tbsp **olive oil**
1 tsp **dried parsley**
3 tbsp **full-fat crème fraîche** or you can use cream cheese, or a mix

100g **smoked salmon**, torn into small pieces or tinned salmon or leftover cooked salmon
juice of ½ **lemon**
black pepper

Cook the pasta in a pan of boiling water according to the packet instructions.

When there are about 3 minutes of the pasta's cooking time left, add the peas.

Once the pasta and peas are cooked, drain them and transfer to a serving bowl. Drizzle with the olive oil and add the parsley.

Stir through the crème fraîche and add the salmon.

Squeeze in the lemon juice and season with a little black pepper before serving.

FREE FROM *(if egg-free fresh pasta is used)*

Variations
You could swap the salmon for leftover roast chicken, or the peas for finely diced green beans.

family dinners

Salmon & Leek Wellington ❄

A Sunday dinner classic in our house. This simple showstopper has become a regular on my meal plan. You can just add some greens on the side, or serve with potatoes, too, if you are feeling hungry.

● ●

Serves
2–3 adults
+ 2–3 little ones

Time
50 minutes

● ● ● ● ● ● ● ● ● ● ● ●

200g **ready-rolled puff pastry**
30g **unsalted butter** or olive oil
1 **shallot**, finely diced
150g **leeks** (about 2 leeks), thinly sliced
1 tsp **dried parsley**
2 tbsp **soured cream** or full-fat crème fraîche or dairy-free alternative
400g **salmon** or trout fillet
milk (any), for brushing
black pepper

Preheat the oven to 220°C (200°C fan), lightly grease a baking tray and remove the pastry from the fridge.

Melt the butter in a saucepan over a medium heat, add the shallot and cook for 3 minutes before adding the leeks. Reduce the heat (be careful – leeks burn easily!) and cook for 10 minutes until completely soft.

Stir in the dried parsley and a pinch of black pepper.

Lay the pastry out flat on a work surface and spread over the soured cream. On one half of the pastry, arrange the cooked leeks and shallot. Place the salmon fillet on top of the vegetables.

Fold over the other half of the pastry – like a book – and lightly press the edges of the pastry together to seal. Make two small slits in the top of the pastry (this will help the Wellington to cook all the way through) and brush a little milk over the pastry.

Place the Wellington on the lightly greased baking tray and bake in the preheated oven for about 40 minutes until the pastry is golden.

● ●

FREE FROM *(if dairy-free alternatives are used)*

Freezing ❄

Slice into portions after cooking, and freeze on a lined baking tray until solid. Transfer to a freezer bag or container and freeze for up to 3 months. To reheat, defrost fully in the fridge overnight then bake in the oven for 15 minutes at 210°C (190°C fan). ❄

Variation

You can make mini versions by slicing your salmon into individual pieces before adding the filling and wrapping in pastry. Just reduce the cooking time to 18–20 minutes.

Lemon & Garlic Baked Cod

With my babies, I found fish had an easier texture for them to manage than meat at first. Babies can very easily eat fish with their gums alone. This one-tray recipe is full of flavour and produces minimal washing up – always a winner. Just serve with your choice of potatoes or rice.

●●●●●●●●●●●●●●●●●●●●●●

Serves
2 adults
+ 2–3 little ones

Time
25 minutes

2 cloves of **garlic**, finely diced
1 tbsp **olive oil**
juice of 1 **lemon**
1 tsp **dried parsley**
4 **cod fillets** (around 500g)
200g **cherry tomatoes**, halved
3 handfuls of **spinach**, finely diced
black pepper

●●●●●●●●●●●●●●●●●●●●●●

Preheat the oven to 210°C (190°C fan).

In a small bowl, mix together the garlic, olive oil, lemon juice, parsley and a pinch of black pepper to make a dressing.

Lay the fish on a large baking tray and scatter the tomatoes around the fish.

Spoon the dressing evenly over the fish and tomatoes, then bake in the middle of the preheated oven for 15 minutes.

Scatter the spinach around the fish, turning it in the tomatoes and juice, then pop back in the oven for another 5 minutes until the fish is cooked through.

Variation

You don't have to use cod; you can use other types of fish instead, as long as you use a similar sized portion – and choose bone-free cuts.

●●●●●●●●●●●●●●●●●●●●●●

FREE FROM

Roast Chicken Pie

I created this recipe under real stress! 10-month-old Felix was tired and hungry, and I needed to get dinner on the table as quickly as I could with limited ingredients. I cut as many corners as possible, balancing the baby on my hip. To my surprise, the end result was amazing. I love the combination of the lemony chicken with the butternut squash.

Serves
2 adults
+ 2–3 little ones

Time
30 minutes

about 500g leftover **roast chicken**, shredded
150g **mushrooms**, grated
1 **courgette**, grated
3 tbsp **full-fat crème fraîche**
1 tbsp **dried parsley**
juice of 1 **lemon**
about 500g **mashed butternut squash** and **potato** (leftovers from your Sunday roast are perfect!)
a handful of grated **Cheddar**
black pepper

Preheat the oven to 230°C (210°C fan).

Place the chicken in a large ovenproof dish along with the mushrooms and courgette.

Stir through the crème fraîche, parsley, lemon juice and a pinch of black pepper.

Spoon the mash evenly over the top. Sprinkle over the grated cheese and bake for about 25 minutes until the cheese begins to crisp.

Leave to cool slightly before serving with your choice of greens.

FREE FROM

Serving Suggestion

You can roll the mash with the pie filling to make this easier for a younger baby to pick up, or just let them tuck in!

Mini Falafel Burgers

These iron-rich chickpea burgers are perfect for meze-style sharing. I like to serve them with tzatziki, pitta and salad veg.

Makes
12

Time
20 minutes
+ 30 minutes chilling

80g **potato** (about
½ potato), peeled
and roughly diced

100g **cauliflower**,
cut into florets

240g tinned or cooked
chickpeas, drained

½ tsp **ground cumin**

1 tsp **garlic powder**

1 tbsp **dried mint**

1 tbsp **tahini**

1 tbsp **sesame seeds**

80g **breadcrumbs**

2 tbsp **olive oil**

Bring a pan of water to the boil, add the potato and cook for 10 minutes, then add the cauliflower to the pan and cook for another 5 minutes until both are soft. Drain and transfer to a large bowl.

Add the chickpeas, cumin, garlic powder, mint, tahini, sesame seeds and three-quarters of the breadcrumbs.

Using a hand blender, blend the mixture until you have a thick paste. Cover and refrigerate for 30 minutes or longer.

Sprinkle the remaining breadcrumbs onto a plate. Heat the oil in a frying pan over a medium heat.

Roll the falafel mixture into balls (about 2 tablespoons per ball) and roll each ball through the breadcrumbs once.

Place the balls in the hot pan (it's important that the oil is hot otherwise the falafel will just soak up the oil) and cook for 2 minutes, before lightly squashing the falafel balls with a spatula to form patties.

Cook for another 3–5 minutes, flipping often, until crispy and golden.

FREE FROM *(if soya-free bread used)*

Variation

You can serve as round falafel balls rather than patties, if you prefer. Alternatively, you can bake them in the oven for 15 minutes at 220°C (200°C fan).

❄ Freezing ❄

Place the cooked falafel onto a lined baking tray and freeze until solid, then transfer to a freezer bag or container and freeze for up to 3 months. To reheat, cook from frozen for 20 minutes at 220°C (200°C fan) until piping hot all the way through.

Hummus & Couscous Chicken Traybake

This is possibly the perfect midweek meal! It's all-in-one, delicious and full of goodness. You could serve as it is or add a minty yoghurt dip and some flatbreads to share.

Serves
2 adults
+ 2–3 little ones

Time
40 minutes

1 small–medium
  aubergine,
  cut into wedges
½ **courgette**,
  cut into sticks
1 **red pepper**,
  cut into sticks
1 tsp **ground cumin**
1 tsp **ground cinnamon**
1 tsp **garlic purée**
2 tbsp **olive oil**
6 skinless **chicken thighs**
6 heaped tsp **hummus**
  (shop-bought or see
  pages 134–136)
40g **couscous**
juice of ½ **lemon**

FREE FROM

Preheat the oven to 220°C (200°C fan).

Place the cut vegetables in a large baking dish (or across two baking trays) and add the spices, garlic purée and 1 teaspoon of the olive oil. Toss everything together to coat in the oil and spices.

Arrange the chicken in the tray and spread 1 teaspoon of hummus onto each chicken thigh.

Sprinkle the dry couscous over the entire dish and drizzle with the lemon juice and remaining olive oil.

Bake in the preheated oven for 30 minutes, or until the juices in the chicken run clear.

Serving suggestion:
To serve the chicken to your baby, slice the chicken thighs into strips once cooked. Older babies can have theirs cut into little pieces.

Pork & Mango Meatballs

My family like to eat these fruity meatballs with pitta, tzatziki, sweet potato wedges and salad. You could also serve some fresh mango alongside, which can help your baby to recognise the flavour – it adds a nice bit of colour to the plate, too!

Serves
2 adults
+ 2–3 little ones

Time
30 minutes

1 small **onion**, finely diced
1 tsp **garlic purée**
1 tsp **ginger purée**
1 tbsp **dried coriander**
70g **mango purée**
500g **pork mince**
40g **breadcrumbs**
1 **egg**

Preheat the oven to 220°C (200°C fan) and lightly grease a large baking tray.

Put the onion in a mixing bowl and add the garlic and ginger purées, coriander and mango purée. Mix everything together with a spoon.

Add the pork mince, breadcrumbs and egg, and combine gently with your hands (alternatively you can use a stand mixer with paddle attatchment).

Tear off small handfuls of the mixture and roll into golf-ball-sized meatballs.

Place the meatballs onto the tray and bake in the preheated oven for 18 minutes until cooked through.

FREE FROM *(if soya-free breadcrumbs used)*

Freezing
Cool before placing the meatballs on a baking tray in the freezer. Once frozen you can transfer them to an airtight container and then freeze for up to 3 months. To reheat, defrost in the fridge overnight, then cook them in a pan over a medium-high heat.

Slow Cooker Beef Stroganoff ❄

Red meat can be a bit challenging for babies to eat as it easily becomes tough. I find that slow cooking helps to keep it soft enough to eat – with or without teeth. Slow cookers can be really useful when cooking for babies, as you can make an entire dish while your baby is napping or happily playing. If your baby gets fussy around dinner time, it's well worth investing in a slow cooker! This is one of my favourite slow-cooked beef recipes. I like to serve it with broccoli and pasta or plain brown rice.

● ●

Serves
2 adults
+ 2–3 little ones

Time
5 hours 45 minutes

● ● ● ● ● ● ● ● ● ● ● ●

500g **stewing beef**,
   cut into strips
1–2 tbsp **plain flour**
1 tbsp **olive oil**
1 **onion**, diced
2 cloves of **garlic**, diced
250ml **low-salt beef stock**
1 tsp **mustard**
1 tbsp **paprika**
200g **mushrooms**, diced
½ bunch of **parsley**,
   finely diced
3 tbsp **soured cream**
   or dairy-free alternative
juice of ½ **lemon**

Coat the beef in 1 tablespoon of the flour.

Heat the oil in a pan over a medium heat and, once hot, add the beef (you will probably need to do this in two batches so you do not overcrowd the pan). Cook for a couple of minutes until browned all over, then tip into a bowl and set aside.

Switch the slow cooker to 'high'. Add the onion, garlic, browned beef, stock, mustard and paprika. Put the lid on and cook for 3 hours.

Add the mushrooms to the slow cooker and cook for a further 2½ hours. If the stroganoff begins to look too watery, mix the remaining flour with a little water to make a paste and gently stir in.

Once the 5½ hours total cooking time is up, switch off the slow cooker. Add the parsley, soured cream and lemon juice. Gently stir together before serving.

● ●

FREE FROM *(if dairy-free
alternative is used)*

Freezing ❄

Freeze in an airtight
container for up to
3 months. Defrost in
the fridge overnight.
Reheat on the hob
until piping hot.

Simple Tomato Pasta ❄

This is a great basic to learn. I recommend batch cooking the sauce and freezing in portions so you always have a back-up meal at the ready. You can also use this as a sauce for chicken or fish.

Serves
2 adults
+ 2 little ones

Time
50 minutes

1 tbsp **olive oil**
1 **red onion**, diced
200g **carrots** (about
   2 carrots), diced
1 clove of **garlic**,
   finely diced
500g **salad tomatoes**,
   diced
150ml **water**
150g **vine-ripened
   cherry tomatoes**,
   diced
400g **pasta**
black pepper
Italian hard cheese
   (optional)

Heat the oil in a pan over a medium heat, add the onion and cook for about 10 minutes until it starts to turn translucent.

Add the carrots and garlic, along with a splash of water, and cook for 5 minutes until beginning to soften.

Add the tomatoes and water to the pan, bring to a simmer, then reduce the heat to low and cook for 35–40 minutes until the tomatoes have completely broken down and the sauce has begun to thicken.

Meanwhile, cook the pasta in a pan of boiling water according to the packet instructions (longer for baby).

Blend the sauce with a hand blender (if you wish!) and season with black pepper and a dot of olive oil.

Mix the sauce with the pasta, or serve on top. Sprinkle over some Italian hard cheese for adults. Alternatively you can store the sauce in the fridge in an airtight container for up to 3 days.

FREE FROM

(if cheese omitted)

Variations

You can do so much with this simple dish! Try adding a spoonful of mascarpone, a few torn basil leaves, some roasted veg, leftover chicken ... lots of possibilities.

Freezing

Freeze in an airtight container for up to 3 months. Defrost in the fridge overnight. Reheat on the hob until piping hot.

Silky Butternut Rigatoni

The best pasta dishes are simple. You should be able to taste every ingredient. Your baby will love the smooth texture and creamy taste of this dish. I like to cook the butternut squash in advance to save time, but I have included the cooking instructions in the recipe if you need them. To add a little more protein to this dish, you could sprinkle over a little cheese or nutritional yeast before serving.

Serves
2 adults
+ 2–3 little ones

Time
25 minutes

400g **butternut squash**, peeled and cut into 1.5cm cubes

400g **rigatoni** or any other pasta

1 tbsp **olive oil**

80g **unsalted butter**

1 **onion**, finely diced

1 tbsp **dried sage**

3 tbsp **full-fat crème fraîche**

juice of ½ **lemon**

black pepper

Bring a pan of water to the boil, add the the squash and cook for about 12 minutes until soft.

Drain most of the water from the squash, keeping back a little of the water for the sauce. Set aside.

Cook the pasta in a pan of boiling water according to the packet instructions (longer for a baby). Drain and stir through the olive oil once cooked.

Meanwhile, melt the butter in a large pan over a medium heat, add the onion and sage, and cook for about 7 minutes until the onion is really soft. You may need to add a splash of water.

Add the cooked squash, reduce the heat to low and cook for about 5 minutes until the butternut squash is falling apart.

Add the crème fraiche and lemon juice, and slowly swirl together.

Gently mix the sauce and pasta together. Season with a little black pepper and serve.

FREE FROM

Mushroom & Tarragon Pasta

This is a quick little dinner that you can scale down for just your baby or serve to the whole family. The sauce is quite strongly flavoured, so a little goes a long way.

●●●●●●●●●●●●●●●●●●●●●●●●●●●

Serves
2 adults
+ 2–3 little ones

Time
15 minutes

●●●●●●●●●●●●●

400g **pasta** (whichever shape you prefer)

20g **unsalted butter** or 2 tbsp **olive oil**

10 **white mushrooms**, diced

1 tsp **garlic purée**

4 tbsp **pine nuts**

2 tsp **fresh tarragon** or parsley

3 tbsp **full-fat crème fraîche** or dairy-free alternative

black pepper

Cook the pasta in a pan of boiling water according to the packet instructions (longer for baby).

Meanwhile, heat the butter or oil in a pan over a medium heat, add the mushrooms and cook for about 3 minutes until they start to soften.

Add the garlic purée and pine nuts and cook for another 1–2 minutes.

Turn off the heat and add the tarragon and crème fraiche, then pulse with a hand blender until smooth. Season with a pinch of black pepper.

Drain the cooked pasta and stir through the sauce.

●●●●●●●●●●●●●●●●●●●●●●●●●●●

FREE FROM *(if dairy-free alternatives used)*

Variation

If you swap the crème fraiche for cream cheese, you'll have a delicious mushroom pâté!

Best Veggie Bolognese

We eat a 'flexitarian' diet at home, so I have done a lot of research into what makes a good meat-free Bolognese! I think mushrooms are the key – the more, the better. The oat milk gives the sauce a luxuriously creamy finish that makes the dish feel pretty close to the real thing, too. Just add pasta!

Serves
2 adults
+ 2–3 little ones

Time
40 minutes

1 tbsp **olive oil**,
    plus extra if needed
1 **onion**, finely diced
1 **carrot**, finely diced
1 clove of **garlic**, finely diced
1 stick of **celery**, finely diced
500g **mushrooms** (I like
    to use a mix of chestnut
    and white mushrooms)
1 **green pepper**, diced
400g **tinned chopped
    tomatoes**
⅔ tsp **yeast extract spread**
    (optional)
1 tsp **dried sage**
2 **bay leaves**
a handful of **basil**, torn
50ml **'whole' oat milk** or
    1–2 tbsp dairy-free cream

FREE FROM

In a large pan, heat the oil over a medium heat, add the onion and cook for about 10 minutes until softened.

Once soft, add the carrot, garlic and celery to the pan and cook for around 5 minutes.

Dice three-quarters of the mushrooms into small pieces and add to the pan with the diced pepper. Cook for 10 minutes, adding extra olive oil or a splash of water if needed.

Add the chopped tomatoes, yeast extract if using, dried sage and bay leaves, and bring to a simmer. Cover with a lid, reduce the heat to low and cook for 15 minutes.

Grate in the rest of the mushrooms (this helps create a more 'meaty' texture). You can add even more mushrooms if you want to!

Cook for another 10 minutes on low, adding a splash of water or low-salt veg stock if needed.

Remove from the heat, remove the bay leaves and stir in the fresh basil and the oat milk.

Freezing
Freeze in an airtight container for up to 3 months. Defrost in the fridge overnight. Reheat on the hob until piping hot.

Very Easy Vegetarian Lasagne ❄

I love lasagne, but I always found it a bit tricky to coordinate cooking all the different parts with babies and toddlers around. This method cuts out a lot of the cooking (and washing up), but tastes really delicious. If you prefer a meaty lasagne, add a layer of cooked beef, pork or turkey mince.

Serves
2 adults
+ 2–3 little ones

Time
50 mins

5 tbsp **tomato purée**

1 tbsp **Italian herbs**

1 tsp **garlic purée**

1 tbsp **olive oil**

250g **fresh lasagne sheets**
(must be fresh, not dried!)

150g **cream cheese**

1 **courgette**

6 **mushrooms**

⅓ **aubergine**

2 handfuls of **spinach**,
finely diced

1 ball of **mozzarella cheese**

Preheat the oven to 220°C (200°C fan).

Mix the tomato purée, Italian herbs, garlic purée and olive oil in a bowl to make the tomato sauce.

Lay a single layer of lasagne sheets on the bottom of a 30 x 20cm ovenproof dish.

Spread over the tomato sauce followed by a spoonful of the cream cheese.

Grate one-third of the courgette, mushrooms and aubergine directly on top and sprinkle over some spinach.

Repeat to create two more layers of pasta, tomato sauce, cream cheese and vegetables, then top with a final layer of lasagne sheets.

Cover with the rest of the cream cheese and then tear over the mozzarella.

Cover the lasagne with foil and bake in the preheated oven for 20 minutes.

Remove the foil and bake for 20 minutes until bubbly and golden. Check it is completely cooked through with a sharp knife.

Leave to cool a little before serving.

Serving suggestion
Deconstruct your baby's portion, so they can pick up individual pieces of pasta. Offer just a little bit at a time.

FREE FROM

Freezing
Freeze portions in airtight containers for up to 3 months. Defrost in the fridge overnight then, bake in the oven for 20 minutes at 220°C (200°C fan).

Creamy Tomato & Courgette Risotto

A fresh but comforting midweek meal that doesn't take too much prep or cooking time. We have this either on its own or alongside a piece of fish.

Serves
2 adults
+ 2–3 little ones

Time
35 minutes

1 tbsp **olive oil** or unsalted butter

350g **cherry tomatoes**, quartered

1–2 cloves of **garlic**, finely diced, to taste

300g **risotto rice**

700ml **low-salt vegetable stock**

250g **courgette** (about 1 courgette), grated

1 tbsp **nutritional yeast** (optional)

2 tbsp **mascarpone** (optional)

8 **fresh basil leaves**

black pepper

Heat the oil or butter in a pan over a medium heat, add the tomatoes and garlic, and cook for 5 minutes.

Add the risotto rice and toss with the tomatoes and garlic for 1 minute.

Add the low-salt vegetable stock (all in one go is fine!), the nutritional yeast (if using) and the grated courgette, then cook for 20 minutes over a low heat, stirring regularly. You may wish to add a little extra water and cook for another 5 minutes if you would like it softer.

Remove from the heat, stir through the mascarpone, tear in the basil leaves and add a little black pepper to finish.

FREE FROM *(if dairy-free alternatives + gf stock used)*

Variation

You can use this recipe to make simple arancini balls by rolling in breadcrumbs and lightly frying.

Serving suggestion

For babies, you can offer on a spoon or let them scoop it up with their hands (often more effective than you might think!) and worry about the mess after!

Simple Beef Bolognese ❄

I like classic Bolognese. I think it tastes better without too many additional herbs and vegetables shoved in for the sake of vegetables. The only non-traditional ingredient here is the sweet potato. I have used this to replace both the sweetness you find in a traditional Bolognese that has been simmering for hours and hours and the added sugar that some recipes call for. The sweet potato also gives the dish a wonderfully silky texture. Serve with fresh spaghetti and Romanesco broccoli.

Serves
2 adults
+ 2–3 little ones

Time
45 minutes

1 tbsp **olive oil**
1 **onion**, finely diced
1 clove of **garlic**, finely diced
1 stick of **celery**, finely diced
200g **sweet potato**,
  peeled and diced
500g **beef mince**
400g **passata**
2 **bay leaves**
150g **mushrooms**,
  diced or grated
50ml **whole milk** or 'whole'
  oat milk
250g **dried spaghetti**
30g **Italian hard cheese**,
  grated

Heat the oil in a pan over a medium heat and add the onion. Cook for 10 minutes until translucent, adding a splash of water if necessary.

Add the garlic, celery and sweet potato, and cook for 3 minutes, then add the beef mince and cook for another 3 minutes until the meat is turning brown.

Add the passata, bay leaves and mushrooms, bring to a simmer, then turn the heat down to low and cook for 35 minutes (or longer if you can), stirring now and then. Add a splash of water if it begins to thicken too much.

While the bolognese simmers, cook the spaghetti for 12 minutes or longer if you prefer a softer texture for your baby.

Remove from the heat and discard the bay leaves. Add the milk and a ladle of pasta water, then serve over spaghetti (or your pasta of choice). Add a sprinkle of Italian hard cheese over adult and big kid's portions.

FREE FROM

Freezing

Freeze in an airtight container for up to 3 months. Defrost in the fridge overnight. Reheat on the hob until piping hot.

Variation

I have also made this with turkey and pork mince — both taste wonderful! You could add a pinch of fennel seeds to a pork mince-based Bolognese.

Mediterranean Fish & Bean Stew

This fish stew is fresh and comforting all at the same time. It is also much cheaper to make than other fish dishes! Serve simply with mashed potatoes and extra greens.

Serves
2 adults
+ 2 little ones

Time
25 minutes

- 1 tbsp **olive oil**
- 1 **onion**, finely diced
- 1 clove of **garlic**, finely diced
- 1 stick of **celery**, finely diced
- 1 **carrot**, finely diced
- 8–10 **cherry tomatoes**, quartered
- 400g **tinned chopped tomatoes**
- 1 tsp **smoked paprika**
- 2 **white fish fillets**, cut into 2cm cubes
- 240g **tinned cannellini beans** or substitute for another white bean
- a handful of **fresh basil**, finely diced or 1 tsp dried
- a handful of **fresh parsley**, finely diced or 1 tsp dried
- a handful of **spinach**, finely diced
- juice of ½ **lemon**
- **black pepper**

Add the oil to a large pan over a medium heat, add the onion and cook for 10 minutes until translucent.

Add the garlic, celery and carrot, and cook for 8–10 minutes until the carrot begins to soften.

Add the cherry tomatoes, tinned tomatoes and smoked paprika, and bring to a simmer.

Add the fish and beans, then cook over a low heat for 10–15 minutes until the fish is just cooked.

Add the herbs, spinach, lemon juice and a pinch of black pepper to the pan. Give it a stir and serve.

FREE FROM

Freezing ❄

Freeze in an airtight container for up to 3 months. Defrost in the fridge overnight. Reheat on the hob until piping hot.

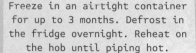

Variation

For an economical fish pie, just top with mashed potato and grated cheese, and bake in the oven for 20–25 minutes at 220°C (200°C fan). You could also add some chorizo crumb (finely diced chorizo) for older babies and beyond.

Beef & Bean Chilli

As well as being yummy, this chilli is full of iron and vitamin C. It isn't spicy, so go ahead and add chipotle or chilli flakes to your own portion, or enjoy the zesty, smokey flavours just as they are. We like to serve chilli with ALL the sides in this house: guacamole or sliced avocado, rice or wraps, soured cream, lime wedges and a sprinkle of cheese.

Serves
2 adults + 2–3 little ones

Time
45 minutes

1 tbsp **olive oil**

1 **onion**, finely diced

1 clove of **garlic**, finely diced

1½ tbsp **smoked paprika**

1 tbsp **ground cumin**

½ tsp **mild chilli powder**

250g **beef mince**

150g **sweet potato** (about 1 sweet potato), diced

1 **yellow pepper**, diced

100g **cherry tomatoes**, diced

150ml **low-salt beef stock**

3 tbsp **tomato purée**

235g **tinned black-eyed beans**

1 **lime**, halved

1 **satsuma**, halved

a small bunch of **fresh coriander**, diced

Heat the oil in a large pan over a medium heat, add the onion and cook for 8–10 minutes until it starts to soften.

Add the garlic and spices, then add the beef mince and cook for a few minutes until browned.

Add the sweet potato, pepper and tomatoes, and cook for another 5 minutes.

Add the stock and the tomato purée, before reducing the heat to low and adding a lid. Cook for 15 minutes.

Add the beans and squeeze in the lime and satsuma (juice and flesh). Add half the coriander to the pan and cook for another 20 minutes on low until the sweet potato and peppers are soft.

Add the rest of the coriander right before serving.

FREE FROM    *(if gf stock is used)*

Freezing

Freeze in an airtight container for up to 3 months. Defrost in the fridge overnight. Reheat on the hob until piping hot.

Sticky Veggie Chilli ❄

This colourful recipe is full of lovely fresh ingredients and doesn't take long to cook at all. It isn't spicy, so just add diced chilli or hot sauce to your own portion. Serve with wraps or rice and guacamole.

• •

Serves
2 adults
+ 2–3 little ones

Time
25 minutes

• • • • • • • • • •

1 medium **sweet potato**

1 tbsp sunflower or rapeseed **oil**, plus extra if needed

1 **onion**, finely diced

1 **yellow pepper**, diced

1 tsp **garlic purée**

1 tsp **ground cumin**

1 tsp **mild chilli powder**

2 tsp **smoked paprika**

200g **tinned kidney beans**, drained

200g **tinned chickpeas**, drained

400g **tinned chopped tomatoes**

a large handful of **spinach**, finely diced

a handful of **fresh coriander**, finely diced

Pierce the sweet potato and microwave on high for 5 minutes, turning once. Set aside.

Heat the oil in a pan over a medium heat, add the onion and cook for about 7 minutes until it starts to soften.

Add the pepper, garlic purée and spices, and cook for 5–10 minutes, adding a little more oil if needed.

Add the beans, chickpeas and chopped tomatoes, and cook on high for 10 minutes.

Carefully peel the sweet potato, cut it into chunks and add to the chilli.

Add the spinach and coriander, and cook on low for a further 5 minutes until the chilli looks thick and sticky.

• •

FREE FROM

Freezing

Freeze in an airtight container for up to 3 months. Defrost in the fridge overnight. Reheat on the hob until piping hot.

Tip

If you don't have a microwave, you can bake the sweet potato instead.

Peanut Butter Noodles

Lots of stir-fry recipes depend on added sugar, honey or lots of salty soy sauce for flavour, which are not suitable for babies. This recipe is full of flavour, but also a lot lower in salt. Feel free to add extra veg if you want to, either in the dish itself or on the side.

● ●

Serves
2 adults
+ 2 little ones

Time
15 minutes

● ● ● ● ● ● ● ● ● ● ● ●

2 heaped tbsp **salt-free peanut butter**

juice of 1 **lime**

1 clove of **garlic**, grated or finely diced

2cm piece **fresh ginger**, grated or finely diced

1 tsp **soy sauce** (just a little; you can add more for grown-ups!)

1 tsp **sesame oil**, plus extra for cooking

100ml **water**

100g **courgette** (about ½ courgette), grated

100g **carrot** (about 1 carrot), grated

80g **mushrooms**, grated

300g **cooked egg noodles**

2 tsp **sesame seeds**

● ● ● ● ● ● ● ● ● ● ● ● ● ● ● ● ● ● ●

FREE FROM

To make the sauce, mix the peanut butter, lime juice, garlic, ginger, soy sauce and sesame oil in a bowl. Add the water and stir to loosen the sauce.

Heat around 1 tablespoon of sesame oil in a wok and add the grated courgette, carrot and mushrooms. Cook for 1–2 minutes until the mushrooms begin to cook.

Add the egg noodles and the sauce, and cook for 3–4 minutes or until the noodles and vegetables are soft. Keep tossing the pan to ensure it cooks evenly.

Remove from the heat and sprinkle over the sesame seeds before serving.

Serving suggestion

Noodles are fun to squish and wiggle, so I like to keep them long for babies. Older babies may prefer them cut up.

Rainbow Coconut Curry ❄

This dish is packed with veg and is very easy to put together, despite the relatively long list of ingredients! It makes enough to feed at least six, so you may have enough to freeze for another day.

● ●

Serves
3 adults
+ 3 little ones

Time
1 hour

● ● ● ● ● ● ● ● ● ●

1 tbsp sunflower
   or rapeseed **oil**
1 **onion**, diced
2 tbsp **curry powder**
1 tsp **ground cumin**
1 tsp **ground cinnamon**
1 tsp **garlic purée**
1 tsp **ginger purée**
1 **sweet potato**,
   roughly diced
about 80g each of
   **butternut squash,
   broccoli, cauliflower,
   aubergine** and **yellow
   pepper**, roughly diced
200g **cherry tomatoes,**
   diced
50g **dried red lentils**
300ml **water**
4 tbsp **tomato purée**
200ml **coconut cream**
a handful of **fresh
   coriander**, diced

Heat the oil in a pan over a medium heat, add the onion and cook for 10 minutes until translucent, then stir in the spices and garlic and ginger purées.

Add all the veg to the pan, along with all the remaining ingredients except the coriander.

Reduce the heat and simmer over a low heat for about 45 minutes, or until the lentils are cooked and the veg is completely soft. You may need to add a little extra liquid.

To finish, stir through the coriander.

Tip
Add diced chillies to the adult portions for an extra kick!

● ●

FREE FROM

Freezing
Freeze in an airtight container for up to 3 months. Defrost in the fridge overnight. Reheat on the hob until piping hot.

Sticky Orange-glazed Salmon

I hope your baby enjoys the subtle Asian flavours in this dish. Salmon is a great source of omega 3, protein and iron, so we try to eat it every week. Try serving this recipe with my Peanut Butter Noodles (see page 126) and some fresh orange wedges.

Serves
2 adults
+ 2–3 little ones

Time
25 minutes
(+ 30 minutes marinating)

500g **salmon fillet**

grated zest and juice
    of 1 large **orange**

1 tsp **sesame oil**

1 tsp **soy sauce**

½ tsp **five spice powder**

Carefully slice the salmon fillet into portions (a 500g piece should easily slice into four or five smaller fillets).

Add the orange zest and juice to an ovenproof dish and mix in the sesame oil, soy sauce and five spice.

Place the salmon portions in the dish, skin-side down in the marinade. Cover and refrigerate, leaving to marinate for at least 30 minutes.

Meanwhile, preheat the oven to 210°C (190°C fan).

Bake the salmon in the centre of the preheated oven for 15 minutes until cooked through.

Pour over a little of the juice and serve immediately.

FREE FROM

Fruity Prawn Korma ❄

Prawn Korma was my favourite meal as a child, and I'm glad that my children love it too! This is a really simple recipe and a great introduction to both curry and prawns. Serve with rice and fresh greens or daal.

Serves
2 adults
+ 2 little ones

Time
15 minutes

1 tbsp sunflower or rapeseed oil, plus extra if needed
1 **onion**, finely diced
1 **yellow pepper**, finely diced
1 clove of **garlic**, finely diced
1 tbsp **garam masala**
1 tsp **turmeric powder**
2 tsp **ground cinnamon**
250g **cooked king prawns**
250g **tinned coconut cream**
70g **mango purée** or a mixed fruit purée containing mango, or finely diced fresh mango

Heat the oil in a large pan over a medium heat, add the onion and cook for a few minutes until it begins to soften.

Add the diced yellow pepper, garlic, garam masala, turmeric and cinnamon, and cook for about 8 minutes until the peppers are soft, adding a little extra oil or a splash of water if needed.

Add the prawns to the pan, stirring to coat them in the vegetable and spice base. Cook for 2 minutes, then add the coconut cream and mango purée, and gently stir in.

Bring to a simmer and cook for just a few more minutes before taking off the heat.

To serve, chop your baby's prawns into small pieces before spooning over the sauce.

FREE FROM

Variation

You could swap the prawns for cooked chicken, turkey, tofu or chickpeas, if preferred.

Freezing ❄

Freeze in an airtight container for up to 3 months. Defrost in the fridge overnight. Reheat on the hob until piping hot.

Serving suggestion

To serve to your baby, butterfly the prawns or chop them really small.

Japanese-style Chicken Curry ❄

This is a really gentle introduction to Japanese-style cooking – the flavours are delicate and the ingredients are likely to be familiar, but the dish still tastes authentic.

Serves
2 adults
+ 2 little ones

Time
30 minutes

400g diced **chicken**
2 tbsp **plain flour**
1 tbsp sunflower
  or rapeseed **oil**
1 **onion**, finely diced
1 **potato**, peeled and diced
1 **carrot**, peeled and diced
1 **sweet potato**, peeled
  and diced
1 tbsp finely diced
  fresh ginger
1 clove of **garlic**, finely diced
1 tbsp **mild curry powder**
400ml **low-salt chicken stock**
⅓ head **broccoli**, diced
80g **mushrooms**, diced
2 tbsp **tomato purée**
80g fresh or frozen **peas**
1 tbsp **soy sauce** (plus
  extra for adults!)

FREE FROM

Coat the chicken thoroughly in the flour.

Heat the oil in a pan over a medium heat, add the onion and cook for 5–6 minutes until it starts to soften.

Add the potato, carrot, sweet potato, ginger, garlic and curry powder. Cook for 5 minutes, adding a splash of water if you need to.

Add the floured chicken and cook until it begins to turn white, then add the chicken stock, broccoli, mushrooms, tomato purée, peas and soy sauce.

Bring to a simmer then cook over a medium-low heat for 20–25 minutes until the veg is all soft and the chicken is cooked through.

Serve over noodles or rice. You can add extra soy sauce or chilli to your own, if you like.

Serving suggestion

You may wish to shred your baby's chicken once cooked, or you can slice the raw chicken into long strips prior to cooking. Rice can be served on a spoon or rolled with some cooked sweet potato.

Freezing ❄

Freeze in an airtight container for up to 3 months. Defrost in the fridge overnight. Reheat on the hob until piping hot.

dips, spreads & sides

Hummus:
- **Chunky Sweet Potato Hummus** 134
- **Roast Tomato Hummus** 136
- **Lemon & Aubergine Hummus** 136

Speedy Ketchup 137

Tzatziki 137

Guacamole 138

Avocado Butter 139

Sweet Potato Butter 139

Pesto:
- **Spinach Pesto** 140
- **Lettuce Pesto** 140
- **Dairy-free Pesto** 140
- **Tomato Pesto** 140

Cheesy Carrot Chips 142

Herby Potato Wedges 142

Spinach & Coriander Flatbreads 143

Smokey Sweet Potato Fries 145

Perfect Mediterranean Roast Veg 146

Perfect Roast Root Veg 148

Minty Potato Salad 149

Rainbow Side Salad 151

Butternut & Couscous Balls 152

Sticky Coconut Rice 154

Cauliflower & Spinach Chickpea Daal 155

Hummus ❄

Hummus has become a baby-food staple over the last decade. Shop-bought options are fine in moderation, but usually quite salty. In these recipes I have replaced the salt with other flavours, though you can always add a little salt to your own portion, if you wish (and it will still be lower sodium than the shop alternative).

FREE FROM

All recipes
make
1 bowl

Time
around
30 minutes

Chunky Sweet Potato Hummus

250g **sweet potato**
1 tbsp **olive oil**
1 sprig **rosemary**
250g **tinned chickpeas**, drained
1 clove of **garlic**, finely diced, or ½ tsp garlic purée
a squeeze of **lemon**
1 tbsp **tahini**

Preheat the oven to 220°C (200°C fan).

Halve the sweet potatoes and coat with 2 teaspoons of the olive oil and the rosemary.

Bake in the preheated oven for about 30 minutes until the skin has puffed up and falls away easily.

Once cool, scrape off the rosemary and scoop the sweet potato flesh into a mixing bowl, discarding the skin.

In a separate bowl, mash the chickpeas, then add to the sweet potato.

Mix in the garlic, lemon juice, tahini and the remaining 1 teaspoon of olive oil.

Roast Tomato Hummus

250g **cherry tomatoes**
1 tbsp **olive oil**
1–2 cloves of **garlic**, finely diced, to taste, or 1 tsp garlic purée
1 tsp **dried oregano**
250g **tinned chickpeas**, drained
1 heaped tbsp **tahini**
juice of ½ **lemon**

Preheat the oven to 210°C (190°C fan).

Place the tomatoes on a baking tray and add the olive oil, garlic and oregano. Give them a good stir to coat in the oil, then cook in the preheated oven for 20 minutes until soft. Leave to cool (you can do this a few hours before).

Blend the roasted tomatoes, chickpeas, tahini and lemon juice using a food processor or hand blender.

Lemon & Aubergine Hummus

200g **aubergine**, roughly diced
2 tbsp **olive oil**
200g **tinned chickpeas**, drained
3 heaped tbsp **full-fat Greek yoghurt**
1–2 cloves of **garlic**, finely diced, to taste, or 1 tsp garlic purée
juice of ½ **lemon**

Preheat the oven to 220°C (200°C fan).

Place the aubergine in an ovenproof dish, drizzle with the olive oil and roast in the preheated oven for 20–25 minutes until soft (you can do this ahead of time) and leave to cool.

Blend the roasted aubergine, chickpeas, yoghurt, garlic and lemon juice using a food processor or hand blender. You can blend until completely smooth or leave a few lumps. (I prefer it this way!)

Speedy Ketchup

One for red-dip-loving toddlers! This is super easy to make and my children have never questioned that it wasn't the shop-bought one.

Makes
1 small dish

Time
2 minutes

2 tbsp **tomato purée**
2 tbsp **apple juice**
a pinch of **paprika**
a pinch of **oregano**

Freezing

You can freeze this in an ice cube tray, popping out a portion and defrosting in the fridge as needed.

Mix all ingredients in a bowl...

...and you're done! Told you it was speedy!

Store covered in the fridge for up to 3 days.

FREE FROM

Tzatziki

This is a family favourite that works well with BBQ dishes, pitta, falafel, kofta... whatever you like! Tzatziki can be made with either dill or mint, so see which your baby prefers.

Makes
1 bowl

Time
10 mins

⅓ **cucumber**, grated
3 heaped tbsp **full-fat Greek yoghurt**
½ tsp **garlic powder**
2 tsp **dried mint**
  or dill

juice of ⅓ **lemon**
1 tsp **olive oil**

Squeeze the grated cucumber with a clean tea towel to remove as much water as you can and then add to a large bowl.

Spoon in the yoghurt and add the garlic powder and mint, stirring well.

Add the lemon juice and stir through the olive oil.

Keep refrigerated for up to 2 days, stirring before serving.

FREE FROM

Guacamole

I serve this with any Mexican-inspired dish, and often add to mealtime buffets. I find that if my girls only eat one thing on the table, it's this!

● ● ● ● ● ● ● ● ● ● ● ●

Makes
1 bowl

Time
5 minutes

● ● ● ● ● ● ● ● ● ● ●

1 large **avocado**,
   roughly diced
1 **salad tomato**,
   roughly diced
½ small **onion**,
   roughly diced
½ tsp **paprika**
juice of ½ **lime**
2 tbsp **full-fat**
   soured cream
1 tsp **olive oil**

● ● ● ● ● ● ● ● ● ● ●

Add all the ingredients to a blender, or a large mixing bowl if using a hand blender.

Blend until you have a smooth paste.

● ● ● ● ● ● ● ● ● ● ●

FREE FROM

Tip

Adults may wish to add a pinch of sea salt or chilli to their portion.

Avocado Butter

This silky-smooth butter can be used in place of normal butter. For a dairy-free version, you can swap the unsalted butter for coconut oil.

Makes
1 small dish

Time
5 minutes

1 **avocado**
½ a **lemon**
50g unsalted **butter**
black pepper

Place the avocado flesh in a blender, or large bowl if using a hand blender.

Add the lemon juice, butter and a pinch of black pepper, and blend until you have a smooth consistency.

Use immediately or store in an airtight container in the fridge for up to 2 days.

FREE FROM

Sweet Potato Butter

The combination of sweet root veg, cinnamon and cream cheese definitely gives me carrot cake vibes! Try it stirred into porridge or on toast.

Makes
1 small dish

Time
35 minutes

1 small **sweet potato**
50g **apple purée**
½ tsp **ground cinnamon**
2 tsp **cream cheese**

Preheat the oven to 220°C (200°C fan).

Bake the sweet potato in the preheated oven for 25–30 minutes until the flesh is soft. Scoop the flesh out of its jacket into a bowl.

Add the remaining ingredients and mix well until smooth.

Use immediately or store in an airtight container in the fridge for up to 2 days.

FREE FROM

Pesto ❄

Homemade pesto is so versatile; spread it over fish before baking, use as a stuffing for chicken, swirl it into pasta, mix it into mash or dip in a breadstick! To make your own, just blend up any of the following sets of raw ingredients using a hand blender or food processor.

Makes
1 small bowl
Time
5 minutes

Spinach Pesto

30g **fresh basil**
30g **spinach**
50g **pine nuts,**
  cashews or
  walnuts or a
  combination

1 clove of **garlic**
juice of ⅓ **lemon**
20g **Italian hard**
  cheese
2 tbsp **olive oil**

FREE FROM

Dairy-free Pesto

40g **fresh basil**
20g **fresh parsley**
juice of ½ **lemon**
1 clove of **garlic**
40g **pine nuts,**
  cashews

or ground
  almonds
3 tbsp **olive oil**
a splash of **plant-based milk**

FREE FROM

Lettuce Pesto

30g **salad leaves**
  or lettuce
30g **ground**
  almonds
20g **fresh basil**
10g **fresh parsley**
1 clove of **garlic**

juice of ½ **lemon**
20g **Italian hard**
  cheese
1 tbsp **olive oil**

FREE FROM

Tomato Pesto

8 **vine-ripened**
  cherry
  tomatoes (you
  can roast for a
  deeper flavour,
  but it isn't
  essential)

½ **shallot**
20g **fresh basil**
1 tbsp **fresh**
  rosemary
30g **walnuts**
20g **Italian hard**
  cheese

FREE FROM

Storing pesto
As these are not as high in salt as other pesto recipes, they need to be eaten within 2 days to ensure they are completely fresh.

Freezing
You can freeze portions in covered ice cube trays ready to pop out when you need it.

Lettuce pesto is great for using up the end of a bag of salad!

Cheesy Carrot Chips

Perfect for serving with my Turkey Goujons (see page 93), or good old fish fingers!

● ● ● ● ● ● ● ● ● ● ● ● ● ● ●

Serves
2 adults
+ 2 little ones

Time
40 minutes

4 **carrots**
1 tbsp **olive oil**
1 tbsp **fine polenta**
1 tbsp grated **Italian hard cheese**
black pepper

● ● ● ● ● ● ● ● ● ● ● ● ● ●

Preheat the oven to 220°C (200°C fan).

Slice the carrots into batons, place on a baking tray and drizzle with two-thirds of the olive oil.

Bake in the preheated oven for 15 minutes, then sprinkle over the polenta, cheese and a pinch of black pepper. Drizzle over the remaining olive oil and mix with your hands.

Return to the oven for another 15 minutes, or until they are crisp on the outside and soft in the middle.

● ● ● ● ● ● ● ● ● ● ● ● ● ●

FREE FROM

Herby Potato Wedges

Try these with the Lemon and Garlic Baked Cod (see page 104), or served with my Speedy Ketchup (see page 137).

● ● ● ● ● ● ● ● ● ● ● ● ● ● ●

Serves
2 adults
+ 2 little ones

Time
50 minutes

1 large **baking potato** (floury types are best), sliced into wedges
½ tsp **garlic purée**
1 tsp **mixed herbs**
1 tsp **plain flour**
1 tbsp **olive oil**

● ● ● ● ● ● ● ● ● ● ● ● ● ●

Preheat the oven to 220°C (200°C fan). Lightly grease a baking tray.

Place the potato wedges in a bowl and add the garlic purée, herbs, flour and olive oil. Mix well with your hands.

Place the wedges on the baking tray and bake in the preheated oven for 40 minutes, or until crisp.

● ● ● ● ● ● ● ● ● ● ● ● ● ●

FREE FROM

Spinach & Coriander Flatbreads ❄

Ideal for scooping up tagines, curry or hummus, or to serve as an alternative to processed bread at lunchtime. These are extremely easy to make!

Makes
6

Time
10 minutes

100g **self-raising flour**
1 tsp **dried coriander**
½ tsp **garlic powder**
½ tsp **ground cumin**
4 heaped tbsp **full-fat yoghurt**
2 tbsp finely diced **spinach**
sunflower oil spray

Add the flour to a mixing bowl and mix in the coriander, garlic powder and cumin.

Add the yoghurt and the spinach. Mix well, first with a spoon, and then by hand, until you have a ball of dough.

Lightly grease a frying pan or crêpe pan (I like to use oil spray to do this) and set over a medium heat.

Break off golf ball-sized pieces of the dough and roughly shape into rounds by hand (this doesn't need to be perfect).

Place the doughy shapes into the hot pan in batches of 3–4 at a time and let the breads cook for about 30 seconds, then squash them down with the back of a spatula and flip them over.

Cook for 3 minutes, flipping regularly, until the flatbreads have brown spots on each side and appear 'dry'.

Slide onto a plate and repeat with the remaining batches until you have used all of the dough. Serve immediately, or store in an airtight container for up to 1 day.

Variation

You can experiment with different flavours here. Try adding some desiccated coconut to make a peshwari naan equivalent. You can also use this as a pizza base by using mixed herbs instead of coriander and cumin.

FREE FROM

Freezing ❄

Cover and freeze for up to 3 months. Defrost overnight in the fridge. You can lightly toast or warm in the oven, if required.

Smokey Sweet Potato Fries

Banish soggy sweet potato chips with this recipe! The key is to cut them fairly thin and make sure your oven is nice and hot.

●●●●●●●●●●●●●●●●●●●●●●●●●●●●

Serves
2 adults
+ 2 little ones

Time
40 minutes

1 large **sweet potato**
1 tsp **smoked paprika**
2 tbsp **olive oil**

●●●●●●●●●●●●●●●●●●●●●●●●●

Preheat the oven to 230°C (210°C fan). Lightly grease a baking tray.

Slice the sweet potato into sticks (no need to peel) and place in a mixing bowl.

Sprinkle over the paprika and drizzle over the olive oil. Mix well with your hands.

Arrange the chips on the baking tray and bake for about 30 minutes, or until crisp on the outside and soft in the middle.

●●●●●●●●●●●●●●●●●●●●●●●●●

FREE FROM

Perfect Mediterranean Roast Veg

This is a good starting point for babies. Soft, simple and nutritious. I definitely recommend roasting vegetables over steaming or boiling. They are less slippery to hold and offer a much more interesting flavour. Here is my basic recipe, followed by some useful seasoning combinations.

● ●

Serves
2 adults
+ 2 little ones

Time
35 minutes

● ● ● ● ● ● ● ●

1 small **aubergine,**
   cut into wedges
1 small **courgette,**
   cut into batons
1 **red pepper,**
   cut into batons
1 clove of **garlic,**
   finely diced
1 tbsp **olive oil**
1 sprig of **rosemary**
1 sprig of **thyme**

Preheat the oven to 220°C (200°C fan).

Place the vegetables on a baking tray, add the garlic and olive oil, and mix well with your hands. Place the rosemary and thyme on top of the vegetables.

Bake in the preheated oven for 30 minutes until all the vegetables are soft but not completely broken down.

● ●

FREE FROM

Instead of rosemary and thyme you could try the following herbs and spices

Cumin	&	Cinnamon
Mint	&	Lemon zest
Paprika	&	Oregano
Garlic	&	Lemon with fresh parsley

Perfect Roast Root Veg

Root vegetables are a popular choice for first foods. Add interest and extra nutrition with olive oil, herbs and spices. Feel free to pick or choose the veg you use depending on what your children like or what you have to hand; the recipe will still work.

Serves
2 adults
+ 2–3 little ones

Time
50 minutes

2 **carrots**, cut into batons
2 **parsnips**, cut into batons
1 **sweet potato**, cut into wedges
¼ **celeriac**, swede or squash, cut into batons
1–2 **cloves of garlic**, finely diced
2 tbsp **olive oil**
1 tsp **dried parsley** or rosemary
black pepper

FREE FROM

Preheat the oven to 220°C (200°C fan).

Place the vegetables on a large baking tray and add the garlic, olive oil and a pinch of black pepper. Mix well with your hands.

Bake in the preheated oven for 45 minutes until the vegetables are soft, turning midway through cooking. You may need to add extra olive oil.

Variations

You can swap the herbs and spices to suit your dish. Indian spiced root veg is nice – just add 1 teaspoon of garam masala.

Minty Potato Salad

This baby-friendly version of the classic potato salad is perfect as a summery side dish or for picnic adventures. This salt-free recipe uses soured cream as the base for the dressing, rather than mayonnaise, which can be high in salt.

● ●

Serves
2 adults
+ 2–3 little ones

Time
20 minutes

400g **baby potatoes**, halved
150ml **full-fat soured cream**
1 tbsp **dried mint**
1 tbsp **pickle liquid** (straight from a jar of American pickles, gherkins, caperberries, etc)
juice of ¼ **lemon**
1 tsp **olive oil**

● ●

Place the potatoes in a pan of water over a high heat, bring to the boil and cook for 15 minutes, or until tender. Drain the potatoes well.

Mix in the soured cream, mint, pickle liquid, lemon juice and olive oil.

Tip into a serving dish and serve warm or cool.

● ●

FREE FROM

Rainbow Side Salad

This is a picky salad that toddlers can help to make – choosing their ingredients, ripping up lettuce or making patterns. Serve alongside other picky bits at lunchtime or use it to add freshness to an 'oven dinner' on busy evenings! Use the ingredients listed or work with your child's favourites. Once you have made the salad, why not name it after them to give them ownership of their cooking!

Serves
1

Time
10 minutes
(longer with help...)

strawberries, quartered

red/purple grapes, quartered

apple, diced
(for babies over 12 months)

lettuce, torn
(for babies over 12 months)

cucumber, diced

cherry tomatoes, quartered

yellow pepper, diced
(for babies over 12 months)

carrot, grated

juice of 1 **tangerine**

a splash of **olive oil**

Mix all the fruits and vegetables together in a bowl.

Squeeze over the tangerine and add a splash of olive oil.

Lightly mix together before serving.

FREE FROM

Variations

Try changing the dressing... You could make mint and yoghurt, a simple vinaigrette, soy sauce and sesame oil, or tahini and lemon juice. Pre-schoolers might like to invent their own dressing – my girls love to do this!

Butternut & Couscous Balls

Like rice, couscous can also be extremely messy! Rolling the couscous with the squash can make a big difference.

Serves
3 little ones

Time
15 minutes

200g **butternut squash** or sweet potato, peeled and cut into 2cm cubes
100g **couscous**
a squeeze of **lemon**
1 tsp **dried mint**

Bring a pan of water to the boil over a medium heat, add the squash and cook for 12 minutes, or until soft enough to mash.

Meanwhile, put the couscous in a bowl and add enough boiling water to just cover the surface. Cover with a plate or lid and leave to soften for 10 minutes.

Drain the butternut squash and mash it in the saucepan with a potato masher.

Add the cooked couscous to the squash, draining off any excess water. Squeeze in a little lemon juice, add the mint and mix together well. Roll into balls to serve immediately.

FREE FROM

Tip
If you ever serve plain couscous, an Instagram follower once told me the best way to clean it is to let it dry and then hoover it up. Genius!

Sticky Coconut Rice

Rice is one of the messier foods you can offer to your baby! Whilst everything can be cleared up, I personally like to minimise 'droppage' where I can. In this recipe, the coconut milk helps the rice to clump together a little, and creates a thicker texture. Less frustrating and more nutritious for baby, less messy for you...

● ●

Serves
2 adults
+ 2 little ones

Time
25 minutes

200g long-grain
　or basmati **rice**
400ml **tinned
　coconut milk**
200ml **water**
grated zest of ½ **lime**

● ●

Rinse the rice well, add to a large saucepan over a medium heat and add the coconut milk and water.

Bring to the boil, then reduce the heat to low, cover with a lid and cook for 15 minutes. Turnoff the heat and leave to stand for 10 minutes.

Stir in a little lime zest and serve immediately, or cover, cool and refrigerate as soon as possible. You can reheat, until piping hot, the next day, but not after that.

● ●

FREE FROM

Variations

To turn this into a meal, add some stir-fried veg and cooked prawns or chicken to the rice.

Serving suggestion

Just pop directly onto your baby's highchair tray or offer on loaded spoons. Its stickier nature means it is also less likely to fall off the spoon!

Cauliflower & Spinach Chickpea Daal

This simple recipe can be served in several ways. As a side dish for a family curry night or as a dip. Alternatively, you can turn it into a warming soup by adding stock or some water.

● ●

Serves   **Time**
2 adults   20 minutes
+ 2 little ones

● ●

50g **potato** (about 1 small potato), diced
100g **cauliflower**, cut into florets
50g **frozen spinach** (about 2–3 blocks)
2 tsp **mild curry powder**
200g **tinned chickpeas**, drained

● ●

Add the potato, cauliflower and frozen spinach to a large pan of water, bring
to the boil over a high heat and cook
for 10 minutes until soft.

Drain the water, then add the curry powder and chickpeas to the pan.

Blend using a hand blender.

● ●

FREE FROM

puddings

Ice Lollies

• •

Perfect for hot days and sore gums! Feel free to play around with the quantities of fruit and milk. You may prefer a more milk-based lolly for a younger baby to minimise sugar, or try making the Smoothie Drops recipe instead.

• •

ALL FREE FROM   *(if dairy-free alternatives are used)*

Tropical Ice Lollies

Makes:
4–6

Time
5 minutes + freezing

150g **mango**, peeled and diced
150ml **coconut milk drink**
juice of ½ **lime**

Add all the ingredients to a blender (or bowl, if using a hand blender) and blend until smooth.

Pour into ice lolly moulds and freeze.

Smoothie Drops

Makes
up to 20 drops

Time
5 minutes + freezing

30ml **milk** (breastmilk, formula, cow's or dairy-free)
30g **fruit purée**

Line a small baking tray with greaseproof paper.

Mix the milk and fruit purée together in a bowl.

Using a small medicine syringe, drop little circles (about 1cm diameter) of the mixture onto the greaseproof paper.

Cover the tray with cling film and freeze.

Once frozen, pop them in a small Tupperware box and offer to baby on hot days or when they have teething pain.

Strawberry Frozen Yoghurt

Makes
4–6

Time
5 minutes + freezing

150g **strawberries**
150g **Greek yoghurt**
or dairy-free coconut yoghurt
a few drops of **vanilla extract**
2 tsp **agave** or maple syrup (completely optional)

Add all the ingredients to a blender (or bowl, if using a hand blender) and blend until you have a smoothie-like consistency.

Pour into ice lolly moulds and freeze.

Most smoothie combinations work well as lollies. Toddlers might enjoy helping to choose ingredients to make their own!

Late Summer Blackberry Lollies

Makes
4–6

Time
15 minutes
+ cooling and freezing

1 **apple** (around 100g), peeled and diced
150g **blackberries** (if wild, make sure they are soaked overnight to get rid of any nasties!)
a few drops of **vanilla extract**
100ml **oat milk** or almond milk

Put the apple in a pan and cover with water. Add the blackberries and vanilla, and cook for 10 minutes, or until the apple is soft. (If your berries are very tart, you could add a tiny bit of fruit syrup or maple syrup.) Leave the fruit compote to cool.

Once cool, add the oat or almond milk and blend in a blender or using a hand blender.

Pour into ice lolly moulds and freeze.

Berry Semifreddo

Your baby will love this almost-ice-cream on sunny days. You can also serve this as a 'whip' by just leaving out the freezing stage.

●●●●●●●●●●●●●●●●●●●●●●●●●●●●●

Serves
2 adults
+ 2–3 little ones

Time
5 minutes
+ 1 hour freezing

150ml **whipping cream**
2 tbsp **full-fat Greek yoghurt**
100g **strawberries**, finely diced
50g **raspberries**, finely diced

●●●●●●●●●●●●●●●●●●●●●●●●●●●●

Whip the cream until thick.

Add the yoghurt and the diced fruit, and whip for another few minutes until thick.

Spoon into a freezer-safe container, cover and freeze for 1 hour for creamy semifreddo; longer if you prefer more of an 'ice'.

Store in the freezer for up to 3 months, removing for 20 minutes prior to serving (do not refreeze).

●●●●●●●●●●●●●●●●●●●●●●●●●●

FREE FROM

Tip

It's very common for babies and toddlers to just want cold fruit and yoghurt in very hot weather. Keep any leftover fruit in the fridge for a cold refresher.

Watermelon, Orange & Lime Medley

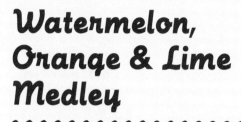

Serve up this delicious fruit salad for a summery pudding or snack. Let your baby enjoy squeezing their own lime juice!

Serves
2 adults
+ 2 little ones

Time
5 minutes

⅓ **watermelon**
2 large **oranges**
juice of 1 **lime**
fresh **mint leaves**
 (optional)

Slice the watermelon into thin slices, then cut in half. It's best to keep the skin on.

Slice the oranges into big wedges, removing any pips.

Squeeze over the lime and scatter over a few mint leaves.

Gently toss together and serve with a yoghurt dip.

FREE FROM

Variation

You could add a very small amount of feta to change this into a delicious side salad!

Mango Mess

This is a tropical sundae-style pudding that the whole family will appreciate. Your baby will enjoy the cloud-like texture of the whipped yoghurt!

● ●

Serves
2 adults
+ 2–3 little ones

Time
5 minutes

5 heaped tbsp **full-fat Greek yoghurt**
½ **mango**, finely diced
2 tbsp **desiccated coconut**
grated zest of 1 **lime** and/or **orange**

● ●

Whisk the yoghurt until it's really thick.

Add the mango and desiccated coconut and whisk in.

Divide between 4–5 little bowls or pots and grate over some orange and/or lime zest.

Serve immediately, or cover and refrigerate for up to 2 days.

● ●

FREE FROM

Variations

For toddlers+, you can use this to top ginger biscuits to make mini cheesecakes!

Summer Pudding

A no-added-sugar version of a British classic. Of course, there is still some sugar in the bread and fruit, so just offer a little portion to your baby. I used a bowl with an 18cm diameter, so choose one as close to that as you can.

● ●

Serves
3 adults
+ 3 little ones

Time
15 minutes
+ 4 hours chilling

400g **frozen mixed summer fruits**
100ml fresh **apple juice**
　　or water if your berries are
　　already quite sweet
10 slices of **white bread**
**Greek yoghurt, cream or dairy-free
alternative** (for serving)

● ●

Line an 18cm pudding basin or medium mixing bowl with cling film.

Add the frozen fruit and juice to a pan over a medium heat.

Simmer for 5 minutes until the berries are fully defrosted and looking sweet and juicy. Leave to cool slightly.

Cut the crusts off the bread and cut in half lengthways, forming little strips of bread.

To line the bowl with the bread, dip rectangles of bread in the berry juice and place all around the sides and base of the bowl (on top of the cling film).

Using the back of a spoon, gently press the berry-soaked bread to the sides of the bowl to ensure the entire bowl is completely lined.

Add another layer of soaked bread in the middle of the bowl, then tip in the remaining berry mixture.

Top with a few more pieces of bread and press the whole thing down with the back of a spoon.

Place a side plate on top of the bowl (it should fit perfectly!)

Refrigerate for at least 4 hours

When you are ready to serve, carefully turn out onto a large plate and peel off the cling film.

Serve immediately with Greek yoghurt, a little whipped cream or a dairy-free alternative, or cover and refrigerate for up to 2 days.

● ●

FREE FROM *(if soya-free bread and dairy-free cream are used)*

Serving suggestion

If your baby can't quite manage to dip the fruit, you can always spread the dip onto the fruit. Older siblings could make fruit kebabs instead.

Fruit Sticks
with Peanut Dip

Puddings can offer a second chance to eat if the main meal wasn't very successful. They can also boost the nutritional content of the meal overall. This mini recipe is packed full of goodness and makes the perfect dessert or snack.

Serves
3 little ones

Time
5 mins

fresh fruit, such as melon, banana, pineapple, mango and large strawberries

1 tbsp **smooth peanut butter**

1 tbsp **full-fat plain yoghurt** or dairy-free alternative

a dash of **fruit juice** or maple syrup (optional)

Slice the fruit into sticks that your baby can pick up and hold.

In a small bowl, mix the peanut butter and yoghurt. Add a dash of fruit juice and mix.

Serve the dip alongside the fruit.

FREE FROM  *(if dairy-free alternative is used)*

Simple Crêpes & Berry Compote ❄

Not just for breakfast, crêpes make a brilliant dessert. Try serving this recipe with a big dollop of thick yoghurt on the side. Makes around 12 crêpes.

● ●

Serves
2 adults
+ 2–3 little ones

Time
10 minutes

● ● ● ● ● ● ● ● ● ● ●

100g **plain flour**
1 **egg**
200ml **whole milk**
   or dairy-free milk
200g **mixed frozen berries**
50–100ml **water**
50ml **apple juice**,
   if needed
sunflower oil spray

Whisk together the flour, egg and milk in a mixing bowl.

Lightly grease a frying pan or crêpe pan (I like to use oil spray to do this) and set over a medium heat.

Ladle in one-sixth of the batter and swirl the pan until the base of the pan is completely covered with a thin layer of batter.

Cook for around 90 seconds. Once the edges begin to lift, slide a spatula underneath to flip it over. Cook the other side for 60–90 seconds.

Repeat with the remaining batter to make five more pancakes. Set aside.

Tip the berries into a saucepan over a medium heat, add the water (and apple juice if the berries are not very sweet), and cook for about 8 minutes until the mixture begins to look 'jammy'.

To serve, you can use the compote to fill the crêpes or serve alongside.

● ●

FREE FROM *(if dairy-free milk is used)*

For lunch or breakfast, you could also try this crêpe recipe with salmon and cream cheese, grated Cheddar and tomatoes, or my Sticky Veggie Chilli (see page 124).

Some flavour options:

Peaches   +   Mascarpone

Banana   +   Peanut butter

Fresh strawberries   +   Whipped cream

Mango (finely diced)   +   Kiwi and melon

Fresh lemon juice *(lots of babies love lemon!)*

Festive Plum Strudel

Full of wintery flavours! You could serve this as an alternative to Christmas Pudding. Enjoy warm with cream or thick, full-fat Greek yoghurt.

Serves
2 adults
+ 2–3 little ones

Time
30 minutes

1 **apple**, diced
2 **plums**, peeled, stoned and diced
300ml **orange juice**
30g **dried cranberries**
a few drops of **vanilla extract**
1 tsp **ground cinnamon**
320g **ready-rolled puff pastry**
milk (any) or egg, for glazing

Preheat the oven to 210°C (190°C fan).

Add the apple and plums to a saucepan with the orange juice, dried cranberries, vanilla extract and cinnamon.

Cook over a high heat for about 10 minutes until the plums and apple are soft and the mixture begins to look sticky.

Cool the fruit mixture (you can do this quickly by spooning into a bowl and carefully resting the bowl in a 'bath' of icy water).

Once the fruit is cool, remove the pastry from the fridge and unroll.

Spread over the fruit mixture, keeping a few centimetres away from the edge.

Carefully roll up the pastry to form a log and make small incisions along the pastry to help it cook evenly.

Brush over a little milk or egg and bake in the preheated oven for 20 minutes.

Leave to cool for 10 minutes before serving. The middle gets very hot!

FREE FROM

(if dairy-free milk is used)

Variation

You can use the fruit mixture as a cranberry sauce alternative at Christmas! Just add extra orange juice and cranberries, then purée until smooth.

Freezing

Cover and freeze the strudel prior to baking (but after cooking the fruit and encasing in pastry). When ready to cook, bake from frozen for 25 minutes at 220°C (200°C fan).

Apple & Peach Crumble ❄

Who doesn't love a good fruit crumble?! This is an all-time favourite pudding in our house, and my girls love helping to make the crumble topping. It's a great workout for tiny hands!

Serves
2–3 adults
+ 2–3 little ones

Time
35 minutes

4 **eating apples**, cored and sliced

227g **tinned sliced peaches** in juice (not syrup)

a few drops of **vanilla extract**

50ml **water**

50g **plain flour**

50g **rolled oats**

50g **unsalted butter** or dairy-free margarine, cubed

Preheat the oven to 210°C (190°C fan).

Place the sliced apples in a pan over a medium heat. Add the tinned peaches along with a couple of spoonfuls of the juice, the vanilla extract and water, and cook for about 8 minutes, or until the apples begin to soften.

Add the flour and oats to a large mixing bowl, add the butter and rub the butter into the flour and oats using your fingertips until you have a crumb-like texture.

Spoon the cooked fruit into an 18 x 25cm ovenproof dish and cover with the crumble topping.

Bake in the preheated oven for 20 minutes until the crumble topping is golden brown.

FREE FROM *(if dairy-free margarine is used)*

Freezing ❄

Cover and freeze prior
to baking (but after cooking
the fruit and topping with
crumble). When ready
to cook, bake from frozen
for 25 minutes at 220°C
(200°C fan).

Variations

Try swapping
the peach for
strawberries,
blackberries
or banana.

Coconut & Date Oat Pots

This recipe was originally a breakfast recipe, but its smoothness and gentle sweetness moves it into the pudding range for me!

● ●

Makes
4–6 pots

Time
5 minutes
+ 4 hours chilling

200ml tinned **coconut milk**
50g **rolled oats**
2 tbsp finely diced **dates**
a pinch of **ground cinnamon**

● ●

Stir the coconut milk well to combine the cream and the water.

Put the oats in a bowl and pour over the coconut milk to cover.

Add the dates and cinnamon, and stir together.

Divide among 4–6 little pots or bowls, cover and refrigerate overnight, or for at least 4 hours. These will keep in the fridge for up to 2 days.

● ●

 **FREE FROM** *(if gf oats are used)*

The pots are quite rich, so I would use baby drinking cups (around 50ml) or washed-out fromage frais pots to make these in.

Baby Panna Cotta

Your baby will enjoy the smooth texture of this low sugar panna cotta. Serve with fresh berries.

● ●

Makes
4–6 pots

Time
5 minutes
+ 4 hours chilling

8g **gelatin powder**
250ml **milk** (any, but I prefer fortified oat milk or coconut milk drink in this recipe)
2 tbsp **double cream** or dairy-free cream
140g peach, mango or apricot **fruit purée**
a few drops of **vanilla extract**

● ●

Dissolve the gelatin in a little hot water by adding the gelatin powder to the water and stirring.

Mix the milk, cream, fruit purée and vanilla in a jug.

Stir in the gelatin mixture.

Pour into little jelly moulds, bowls or ramekins, cover and refrigerate for at least 4 hours before turning out.

Serve immediately, or cover and refrigerate for up to 2 days.

● ●

FREE FROM *(if dairy-free alternatives are used)*

Mini Pear Tarts

You may have noticed that I love to cook with fruit purée! More often than not I just use commercially available pouches, because it's so much easier. On their own, the pouches are actually pretty high in sugar, so why not spread them out over a whole recipe and create something interesting! These little tarts could not be easier to make.

Makes
12

Time
20 minutes

150g **ready-rolled shortcrust pastry**
1 **egg yolk**
70g **pear purée**
a pinch of **ground cinnamon**

Preheat the oven to 210°C (190°C fan). Grease a 12-hole mini muffin tin or petit four tin.

Unroll the pastry and cut out 12 pastry circles. Place them in the tin.

In a mixing bowl, whisk the egg yolk into the pear purée. Spoon the mixture into the pastry cases (you may have a little spare).

Bake in the preheated oven for 10–12 minutes until the custard has set.

Sprinkle over a little cinnamon.

FREE FROM *(if dairy-free pastry used)*

Variations

You can use apple purée instead of pear. For Christmas baking, try adding finely diced mixed fruit and a sprinkle of cinnamon for a mince pie alternative.

Vanilla Semolina Pudding

Semolina pudding is an old-school baby-food classic. Smooth and simple tasting, it's still a useful recipe for tired-out toddlers and teething babies. You can top with fresh fruit or fruit compote, or just serve as it is.

● ●

Serves
2 adults
+ 2 little ones

Time
10 minutes

650ml **whole milk** or dairy-free milk, breastmilk or formula

3 drops of **vanilla extract**

80g **fine semolina**

● ●

Add the milk and vanilla to a saucepan and set over a low heat.

Stir in the semolina and cook, stirring continuously, for around 3 minutes.

When the semolina begins to thicken, turn off the heat and continue to stir for another minute until you have the desired consistency.

● ●

FREE FROM *(if dairy-free milk is used)*

Tip
Semolina is usually found in the 'boxed desserts' section of the supermarket, near the custard powder and jelly.

Classic Rice Pudding

Enjoy this school dinner classic warm or cold. If you have any left over, serve it up as a quick breakfast the next day!

● ●

Serves
2 adults
+ 2 little ones

Time
40 minutes

● ● ● ● ● ● ●

80g **pudding rice**
550ml **whole milk**
  or 'whole' oat
  milk
a few drops of
  vanilla extract
a pinch of
  cinnamon
1–2 tsp **maple
  syrup** or fruit
  syrup (optional)

Add the rice, milk, vanilla extract and cinnamon to a saucepan over a high heat.

Heat until it begins to bubble, then reduce the heat to low and simmer for 30 minutes, stirring occasionally and checking the liquid levels to prevent burning (add more milk you need to).

Remove from the heat and leave to cool a little.

Add the maple syrup, if using.

Once cool enough to serve, top with fresh fruit or fruit purée/compote, if you wish.

● ●

FREE FROM *(if dairy-free milk is used)*

Two-minute Chocolate Orange Pots

Sweetened by only dates and fresh orange, this speedy dessert is a delicious alternative to sugary chocolate puddings. Perfect for toddlerhood and beyond!

Serves
2 adults
+ 2 little ones

Time
2 minutes

1 **tangerine**
2 tbsp diced **dates**
14 tbsp **full-fat Greek yoghurt**
1 tsp **cocoa powder**

Zest the tangerine into a mixing bowl, reserving a little to decorate, if you like.

Add the dates, yoghurt, juice and flesh of the tangerine and the cocoa.

Blend together using a hand blender.

Spoon into little dishes and sprinkle over the reserved zest, if you like.

Serve immediately, or cover and refrigerate for up to 2 days.

FREE FROM

Variation
Try swapping the tangerine for fresh raspberries.

bake together

Tomato, Courgette & Basil Muffins

These tasty muffins are great for picnics and lunchboxes, and they freeze well too. Try them on their own or spread with a little butter, like a scone.

● ●

Makes
12 muffins

Time
30 minutes

● ● ● ● ● ● ● ● ● ● ● ●

100g **cherry tomatoes**,
   finely diced
a handful of **fresh basil
   leaves**, finely diced
3 **eggs**
50g **courgette**, grated
50g **unsalted butter**,
   softened
120g **self-raising flour**
1 tsp **garlic purée**
30g **Cheddar**, grated
a pinch of **black pepper**

Preheat the oven to 220°C (200°C fan) and lightly grease a 12-hole muffin tin.

Put the tomatoes and basil into a large mixing bowl and whisk in the eggs.

Add the grated courgette and butter, and thoroughly mix in the softened butter.

Gently fold in the flour, garlic purée, cheese and black pepper.

Divide the mixture evenly between the holes of the muffin tin and bake in the preheated oven for 18 minutes, or until a skewer inserted into a muffin comes out clean. The muffins should be slightly shiny on top.

Enjoy warm or allow to cool and store in an airtight container in the fridge for up to 24 hours.

● ●

FREE FROM

Tip
It's best not to use cupcake liners with savoury muffins, as they can stick to the paper. If you grease the tin they should come out much more easily.

Freezing
Freeze on a baking tray, then pop in a freezer bag. Defrost in the fridge overnight.

Sweet Potato Muffins

This was one of the first recipes I developed for the Baby Led Kitchen app. I must have made these thousands of times! They freeze beautifully, so they are perfect for pulling out of the freezer for lunchboxes or picnics.

Makes
12 muffins

Time
30 minutes

150g **cooked sweet potato** (I just roast a medium sweet potato whole and scoop out the middle, but you can also use leftover sweet potato mash)
3 **eggs**
50g **unsalted butter**, softened
150g **self-raising flour**
1–2 tsp **smoked paprika**
30g **mature Cheddar**, grated

FREE FROM

Preheat the oven to 230°C (210°C fan) and grease a 12-hole muffin tin.

Mash the sweet potato in a large mixing bowl using a potato masher or fork.

Whisk in the eggs and butter.

Sift in the flour and add the paprika, then stir through the grated cheddar.

Divide the mixture evenly between the holes of the muffin tin and bake in the preheated oven for 15–18 minutes until a skewer inserted into a muffin comes out clean.

Allow to cool, then serve, or store in an airtight container in the fridge for up to 24 hours.

Variations

These muffins work with butternut squash, parsnip, carrot, swede or a combination.

Freezing

Freeze on a baking tray, then pop in a freezer bag. Defrost in the fridge overnight.

The Best Broccoli Muffins ❄

There are so many broccoli muffin recipes out there, and I have tried many different combinations myself! But this is my original, and favourite, recipe. They are really fresh tasting, light in texture and much lower in salt than other recipes out there. I hope you like them, too!

Makes
12 muffins

Time
30 minutes

150g **self-raising flour**
3 **eggs**
60g **unsalted butter**, softened
100g **broccoli**, grated
⅓ tsp **garlic powder**
1 tsp **dried basil**
1 tsp **dried oregano**
juice of ½ **lemon**
30g **Italian hard cheese**, grated

Preheat the oven to 220°C (200°C fan) and lightly grease a 12-hole muffin tin.

Sift the flour into a large mixing bowl and whisk in the eggs and butter.

Add the broccoli, garlic powder, herbs, lemon juice and cheese, and mix gently.

Divide the mixture evenly between the holes of the muffin tin and bake in the preheated oven for 15–18 minutes, or until a skewer comes out clean.

Allow to cool, then serve, or store in an airtight container in the fridge for up to 24 hours.

FREE FROM

Freezing
Freeze on a baking tray, then pop in a freezer bag. Defrost in the fridge overnight.

Courgette & Apple Sconelets ❄

Not quite a scone, not quite a biscuit. This is a great recipe for cooking with toddlers and older children. Little hands will enjoy squeezing the cubes of butter between their fingers, squishing the mixture together, helping to roll the pastry and cutting out the circles. You can do the boring chopping, grating and lifting in and out of the oven, of course.

● ●

Makes
12

Time
30 minutes
+ 1 hour chilling

● ● ● ● ● ● ● ● ● ●

100g **courgette**, grated
   (about 1 courgette)
150g **apple**, grated
   (about 1 apple)
200g **self-raising flour**,
   plus extra for dusting
50g **unsalted butter**,
   cubed
40g **Cheddar**, grated
a splash of **milk** (any),
   for brushing

Squeeze the grated courgette and apple with kitchen paper or a cloth to remove any excess water, then add to a bowl.

Add the flour to the mixing bowl, followed by the butter and cheese.

Work the butter into the mixture with your hands, rubbing it in with your fingertips, then combine the ingredients by hand until you have a ball of dough.

Wrap in greaseproof paper and refrigerate for at least 1 hour.

When you are ready to cook, preheat the oven to 200°C (180°C fan) and line a baking tray with greaseproof paper.

Roll out the dough on a floured surface and cut out circles using an 8cm cutter. Place on the baking tray and brush a very small amount of milk over the top.

Bake in the preheated oven for 15 minutes until the sconelets are golden brown.

Serve warm or cold, or store in an airtight container in the fridge for up to 24 hours.

● ●

FREE FROM

Freezing ❄️

Freeze on a baking tray,
then pop in a freezer bag.
Defrost in the fridge
overnight.

Lemon & Herb Scones

These are really lovely served with soup or simply spread with butter. The mixture is a little stickier than a traditional scone, but they are beautifully soft when cooked!

• •

Makes
12

Time
25 minutes

• • • • • • • • • • • •

200g **self-raising flour**
50g **unsalted butter**, cubed
150ml **whole milk**, plus
    extra for brushing
1 tsp **lemon juice**
1 tsp **Italian hard cheese**,
    grated
1 tsp **mixed herbs**

Preheat the oven to 220°C (200°C fan) and line a baking tray with greaseproof paper.

Sift the flour into a large mixing bowl, add the butter and rub it into the flour using your fingertips.

Add the milk, lemon juice, cheese and herbs, and work together with your hands until the mixture forms a sticky ball.

With clean hands, pinch off small amounts of the mixture (around 1 tablespoon) and place on the tray (they won't be perfectly round – that's fine!).

Brush with a little milk and bake in the preheated oven for 15 minutes, or until they are just starting to turn golden.

Allow to cool and serve, or store in an airtight container in the fridge for up to 24 hours.

• •

FREE FROM

Freezing
Freeze on a baking tray, then pop in a freezer bag. Defrost in the fridge overnight.

Tip
The mixture is quite sticky, so have a bowl of soapy water ready for gooey fingers!

Carrot & Sesame Flapjack

This recipe is so more-ish! One square is never enough! Don't attempt to eat until it is cool though, as it will crumble. Serve with some veggies for your baby's lunch or as a snack for you and your toddler.

● ●

Makes
12 squares

Time
40 minutes

● ● ● ● ● ● ● ● ● ● ● ●

120g **carrot** (about 1 large carrot), grated

120g **rolled oats**

80g **unsalted butter**, softened slightly

50g **Cheddar**, grated

1 tsp **paprika**

2 tbsp **sesame seeds**

Preheat the oven to 210°C (190°C fan) and line a 20cm square tin with greaseproof paper.

Put the grated carrot into a bowl and add the oats and the butter. Work together by hand, rubbing in the butter until it is all incorporated.

Add the cheese, paprika and half the seeds, and continue to knead and squeeze until you have a ball of dough.

Press the mixture evenly into the lined tin and sprinkle over the remaining seeds.

Bake in the preheated oven for about 25 minutes until golden brown.

Leave to cool in the tin before slicing into squares and serving.

● ●

FREE FROM  *(if gf oats are used)*

Storing

Best eaten within a day. Store in an airtight container in the fridge.

Cheesy Butternut Biscuits ❄️

Cheese crackers are a classic toddler snack! These are suitably 'cheesy', but also have lots of extra goodness from the squash. The recipe makes around 15–20 biscuits, depending on your cookie cutter.

●●●●●●●●●●●●●●●●●●●●●●●●●●●●●●●●●

Makes
15–20 biscuits

Time
30 minutes

70g **cooked butternut squash** (excess water removed with kitchen paper)

150g **plain flour**, plus extra for dusting

30g **unsalted butter**, cubed

50g **cheddar**, grated

1 tsp **dried rosemary**

a splash of **milk**

●●●●●●●●●●●●●●●●●●●●●●●●●●●●●●●

Preheat the oven to 220°C (200°C fan) and line a baking tray with greaseproof paper.

Mash the squash in a bowl with a fork or potato masher.

Put the flour in a separate bowl, add the butter and rub the butter into the flour using your fingertips.

Add the butternut squash, grated Cheddar and dried rosemary, and work the ingredients together until you have a ball of dough. If it is too stiff, add a drop of milk.

Turn the pastry out onto a floured surface and roll out to a thickness of about 1cm.

Cut out shapes using cookie cutters (stars, hearts, circles...) and arrange them on the lined baking tray.

Brush with a little milk, then bake for about 15 minutes until crisp and golden.

Allow to cool, then serve, or keep in an airtight container in the fridge for up to 24 hours.

●●●●●●●●●●●●●●●●●●●●●●●●●●●●●●●

FREE FROM

Freezing ❄

Freeze on a baking tray,
then pop in a freezer bag.
Defrost in the fridge
overnight.

❄

Coconut Biscuit Shapes

Young children love to roll out pastry and cut out shapes. To help them to safely reach worktops, it may be worth investing in a 'kitchen helper' – a safe step for children to stand on. This recipe happens to be very low in sugar and dairy-free, too! For a rainy-day activity, older children might enjoy making some colourful icing to decorate their biscuits.

●●●●●●●●●●●●●●●●●●●●●●●●●●●●●●●●●●●

Makes
10–15 biscuits

Time
25 minutes

50g **plain flour**
50g **desiccated coconut**
1 tbsp **solid coconut oil**
50ml **coconut milk drink**

●●●●●●●●●●●●●●●●●●●●●●●●●●●●●●●●●●●

Preheat the oven to 210°C (190°C fan). and line a baking tray with greaseproof paper.

Combine all the ingredients in a bowl until they roll into a ball.

Roll out the pastry thinly and cut out circles (or shapes) using an approximately 8cm cookie cutter. Place them on the baking tray.

Bake in the preheated oven for 12 minutes until they are just starting to turn golden.

Allow to cool and serve immediately, or store in an airtight container for up to 24 hours.

●●●●●●●●●●●●●●●●●●●●●●●●●●●●●●●●●●●

FREE FROM

Berry Nice Coconut Ice

Not the sugar-laden kind, but still delicious and very allergy-friendly. You can use any soft berry in this recipe, but diced strawberries and blueberries are my favourite. This is another simple recipe that your toddlers can easily help with.

● ●

Makes
12 squares

Time
30 minutes

2 large, ripe **bananas**
150g **desiccated coconut**
a large handful of
  diced **berries**

● ●

Preheat the oven to 210°C (190°C fan) and line a 20cm square baking tin with greaseproof paper.

Mash the bananas in a mixing bowl using a fork.

Add the desiccated coconut and the berries, and mix well.

Tip the mixture into the tin and level with a fork (your little one might like to help to 'rake' patterns into the mixture).

Bake in the preheated oven for 15–20 minutes until it begins to change colour just a little.

Leave to cool completely in the tin, before removing from the tin and slicing into squares. Serve, or store in an airtight container in the fridge for up to 2 days.

● ●

FREE FROM

Toddler Oatie Bars ❄

Babies under 12 months don't need snacks, as they should be having milk feeds in between meals. As your baby turns into a toddler, you can begin to offer a couple of light snacks. Oatie bars aimed at young children are expensive, but you can make similar bars at home for much less money. Here are a few different flavours you can bake together.

● ● ● ● ● ● ● ● ● ● ● ● ● ● ● ● ● ● ●

ALL FREE FROM   *(if gf oats are used)*

Makes
12 bars

Time
30 minutes

Juicy Forest Bars

150g frozen **forest fruits**
200ml **red grape juice**
150g **rolled oats**
4 tbsp **sunflower oil**

Preheat the oven to 210°C (190°C fan) and line a 900g/2lb loaf tin with greaseproof paper.

Add the frozen forest fruits and grape juice to a pan over a medium heat and cook for around 5 minutes until the berries are fully defrosted and squashy.

Add the oats to a mixing bowl and mix in the berries and juice.

Add the sunflower oil and mix well.

Transfer the mixture to the lined loaf in and press down with the back of a spoon.

Bake in the preheated oven for 20 minutes, then leave to cool in the tin before turning out of the tin and removing the paper.

Slice into six bars, and then slice each bar in half to make 12 small rectangles or squares. Store in an airtight container for 2 days.

Sunshine Bars

1 **banana** (about 100g
   peeled weight)
70g each **mango** and
   pineapple, finely diced or,
   if easier, use 140g of either
   mango or pineapple
2 **dried apricots**, finely diced
120g **rolled oats**
2 tbsp **sunflower oil**
120ml **coconut milk drink**
1 tsp **ground cinnamon**

Preheat the oven to 220°C (200°C fan) and line a 900g/2lb loaf tin with greaseproof paper.

Mash the banana in a mixing bowl with a fork, and add the rest of the fruit. Add the oats, sunflower oil, coconut milk and cinnamon, and mix well.

Transfer the mixture to the lined loaf in and press down with the back of a spoon.

Bake in the preheated oven for 25 minutes, then leave to cool in the tin before turning out and removing the paper.

Slice into six bars, and then slice each bar in half to make 12 small rectangles or squares. Store in an airtight container for 2 days.

Raspberry & Pear Bars

100g **pear**, peeled and cored
   (ripe enough to mash)
   or use pear purée
120g **raspberries** or you
   could use strawberries
120g **rolled oats**
4 tbsp **sunflower oil**
30g **ground almonds**
a pinch of **ground ginger**

Preheat the oven to 210°C (190°C fan) and line a 900g/2lb loaf tin with greaseproof paper.

Mash the pear in a mixing bowl using a fork and add the raspberries, oats, sunflower oil, ground almonds and ginger. Mix well.

Transfer the mixture to the lined loaf in and press down with the back of a spoon.

Bake in the preheated oven for 18 minutes, then leave to cool in the tin before turning out of the tin and removing the paper.

Slice into six bars, and then slice each bar in half to make 12 small rectangles or squares. Store in an airtight container for 2 days.

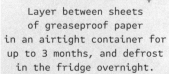

Freezing ❄

Layer between sheets of greaseproof paper in an airtight container for up to 3 months, and defrost in the fridge overnight.

Apple & Cinnamon Flapjack

Another great recipe to bake with your little helpers. There are only a few ingredients and you can mix it up directly in the tin to save on washing up! Suitable for older babies and up.

● ●

Makes
12 squares

Time
25 minutes

● ● ● ● ● ● ● ● ● ● ●

80g **unsalted butter**
   or dairy-free margarine
200g homemade
   apple purée (see below)
150g **jumbo oats**
1 tsp **ground cinnamon**
a large handful of
   sultanas

Grease a 20cm square cake tin.

Melt the butter then transfer it to the cake tin.

Add the apple purée, oats, cinnamon and sultanas, and mix together in the tin.

Press down evenly in the tin, then bake in the preheated oven for 20 minutes until slightly crisp.

Leave to cool completely in the tin, before removing and slicing into squares. Serve, or store in an airtight container for up to 2 days.

● ●

FREE FROM *(if dairy-free margarine and gf oats are used)*

Homemade Apple Purée
● ●

Place 3 peeled and diced **apples** (about 200g) in a saucepan over a high heat, add 1 teaspoon **cinnamon** and just enough **water** to cover, and bring to a boil. Reduce the heat to low and simmer for about 15 minutes, or until the apples are soft and the water has mostly evaporated. Mash with a potato masher or blend in a blender, depending on your preference. Use immediately, or store covered in the fridge for up to 2 days.

Mini Banana Currant Buns ❄️

These easy and allergy-friendly little buns are ideal for older babies and toddlers. The recipe came about during lockdown, when I was desperately trying to balance housework and cooking with entertaining and educating the children! Cooking with very young children offers so many opportunities for playful learning. With this recipe, you could try singing the song together and counting the buns.

Makes
12 small cakes

Time
25 minutes

- 120g **banana** (about 1 large banana)
- 100g **self-raising flour**
- 30g **currants/raisins** (about a handful)
- 120ml **whole oat milk**
- 1½ tbsp **sunflower oil**
- 2 pitted **cherries**, finely diced (optional)

Preheat the oven to 210°C (190°C fan) and grease a 12-hole mini muffin tin.

Mash the banana in a large mixing bowl.

Mix in the flour and the currants, then pour in the milk and sunflower oil and mix together.

Divide the mixture among the holes of the mini muffin tin.

Pop a little piece cherry on the top of each uncooked cake (if using) and bake in the preheated oven for 15 minutes.

Leave to cool completely before carefully removing from the tin.

Serve immediately, or store in an airtight container for up to 24 hours.

FREE FROM

'Five currant buns in a baker's shop, round and fat with a cherry on the top, along came mummy with a penny one day, bought a currant bun and took it away!'

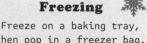

Freezing ❄️
Freeze on a baking tray, then pop in a freezer bag. Defrost in the fridge overnight.

Baby Banana Bread ❄

I have tried many different banana bread recipes over the years but this is our favourite! Naturally sweet, not too cakey and not too crumbly. Enjoy it as it is or toasted, with butter or without. I often toast the very last bit and top it with peanut butter for a pre-bedtime snack for my little ones (and me!).

● ●

Makes
1 loaf (8–10 slices)

Time
55 minutes

● ● ● ● ● ● ● ● ● ●

250g **bananas** (about
  2–3 bananas)
2 tbsp diced **dates**
1 tsp **ground cinnamon**
  or mixed spice
1 large **egg**, beaten
3 tbsp **sunflower oil**
200g **self-raising flour**

Preheat the oven to 210°C (190°C fan) and line a 900g/2lb loaf tin with greaseproof paper.

Mash the bananas really well in a large mixing bowl using a fork.

Squash the dates with the back of a spoon and add to the mashed bananas.

Mix in the cinnamon, then whisk in the egg and the oil.

Sift in the flour and gently mix, taking care not to overmix.

Pour the mixture into the lined loaf tin and bake in the preheated oven for 45 minutes.

Check that the middle is cooked by inserting a skewer – it should come out clean.

Leave in the tin for at least 15 minutes to rest before removing from the tin.

Serve immediately, or store in an airtight container for up to 2 days.

● ●

FREE FROM

Freezing

Freeze after cooking.
Defrost in the fridge
overnight. You can lightly
toast the banana bread to
warm it if you like.

Variations

A handful of chocolate
chips makes a nice
addition for older
children.

Milk Loaf ❄

Bread for babies can be tricky to navigate. Lots of shop-bought varieties are high in salt, making it tricky to fit into the salt recommendation of less than 1g a day for babies under 12 months. Whilst salt is needed to activate the yeast, it is possible to make bread that is much lower in salt than shop-bought alternatives. This recipe produces a fluffy, creamy white loaf with a nutritional boost from the milk.

● ●

Makes
1 loaf (8–10 slices)

Time
2 hours

● ● ● ● ● ● ● ● ● ●

3.5g **fast-action yeast**
(about ⅔ tsp)
350g **strong white flour**
a small pinch of **salt**
170ml **whole milk** or
'whole' oat milk
1 tbsp **olive oil**

Freezing ❄

Pop in a freezer bag and freeze for up to 3 months. Defrost overnight.

❄

Mix the yeast with the flour and a pinch of salt in a large mixing bowl.

Warm the milk slightly, to a little more than room temperature, in a pan on the hob.

Make a well in the flour and pour in the milk and oil, then mix with your hands to bring it together into a ball (it will be slightly sticky).

Place in a lightly oiled bowl, cover with a tea towel and leave in a warm place for at least 1 hour, until it has risen by about half it's size (this bread will rise a little less than a conventional bread dough).

Meanwhile, preheat the oven to 220°C (200°C fan) and lightly grease a 900g/2lb loaf tin.

Tip the dough into the tin and bake in the preheated oven for about 30 minutes until the bread has risen in the tin and has a golden crust.

Leave to cool slightly in the tin before removing from the tin and cooling completely.

Serve warm with a little butter (heavenly!) or leave to cool, wrap and keep in a cool place.

● ●

FREE FROM   *(if dairy-free milk is used)*

Strawberry & Vanilla Muffins

These squishy little muffins are light, fluffy and perfect for taking to toddler play dates. They freeze brilliantly, too – just take out of the freezer the night before you need them to let them defrost (no need to reheat).

●●●●●●●●●●●●●●●●●●●●●●●●●●●●●●●●●●●●●●●

Makes
9

Time
35 minutes

●●●●●●●●●●●●●

2 large **egg** whites
100g ripe **strawberries**, diced
60g **unsalted butter**, softened, or dairy-free margarine
a few drops of **vanilla extract**
100g apple, pear or peach **fruit purée**
30g **ground almonds**
150g **self-raising flour**
1 tbsp **fruit syrup** or honey (for over ones, completely optional)

Preheat the oven to 220°C (200°C fan) and grease a 12-hole cupcake tin.

Whisk the egg whites using a hand-held electric whisk until you have a thick foam.

Add the strawberries, butter, vanilla and fruit purée, and very gently mix through.

Fold in the almonds and flour without overmixing (keep the air in). At this stage you can add a small amount of fruit syrup if serving to over ones.

Divide the mixture between 9 holes of the greased cupcake tin, and bake in the preheated oven for 15–18 minutes until the muffins spring back when you press them, but are still quite pale in colour.

Leave to cool completely in the tin before removing. Serve immediately, or store in an airtight container in the fridge for up to 24 hours.

●●●●●●●●●●●●●●●●●●●●●●●●●●●●●●●●●●●●●●●

FREE FROM *(if dairy-free margarine is used)*

Freezing

Freeze on a baking tray, then pop in a freezer bag. Defrost in the fridge overnight.

Blueberry Fromage Frais Cakes

This is my absolute favourite recipe to bake with my girls. The recipe calls for five little pots of fromage frais, but I usually get six out of the fridge knowing that at least a few spoonfuls will be snaffled! The fromage frais does contain sugar, but you could always use a low-sugar variety for babies.

Makes
12 squares

Time
30 minutes

40g **self-raising flour**
½ tsp **baking powder**
100g **semolina**
3 **eggs**
5 x 45g pots of **fruit-flavoured fromage frais**
1 tbsp **sunflower oil**
a few drops of **vanilla extract**
80g **blueberries**
(I use frozen)

Preheat the oven to 200°C (180°C fan). Line a 20cm square baking tin with greaseproof paper.

Mix the flour, baking powder and semolina in a large bowl.

Whisk the eggs in another bowl and then add all of the fromage frais to the eggs.

Add the egg and fromage frais mixture to the dry ingredients and whisk well.

Add the oil and vanilla, mix well, then gently stir through the blueberries.

Pour the cake mixture into the lined tin and bake in the preheated oven for 20 minutes.

Leave to cool before slicing into squares.

Serve immediately, or store in an airtight container in the fridge for up to 24 hours.

FREE FROM

Freezing
Freeze on a baking tray, then pop in a freezer bag. Defrost in the fridge overnight.

Conversions

Weights

Metric	Imperial
15 g	½ oz
25 g	1 oz
40 g	1½ oz
50 g	2 oz
75 g	3 oz
100 g	4 oz
150 g	5 oz
175 g	6 oz
200 g	7 oz
225 g	8 oz
250 g	9 oz
275 g	10 oz
350 g	12 oz
375 g	13 oz
400 g	14 oz
425 g	15 oz
450 g	1 lb
550 g	1¼ lb
675 g	1½ lb
900 g	2 lb
1.5 kg	3 lb
1.75 kg	4 lb
2.25 kg	5 lb

Volume

Metric	Imperial
25 ml	1 fl oz
50 ml	2 fl oz
85 ml	3 fl oz
150 ml	5 fl oz (¼pint)
300 ml	10 fl oz (½ pint)
450 ml	15 fl oz (¾ pint)
600 ml	1 pint
700 ml	1¼ pints
900 ml	1½ pints
1 litres	1¾ pints
1.2 litres	2 pints
1.25 litres	2¼ pints
1.5 litres	2½ pints
1.6 litres	2¾ pints
1.75 litres	3 pints
1.8 litres	3¼ pints
2 litres	3½ pints
2.1 litres	3¾ pints
2.25 litres	4 pints
2.75 litres	5 pints
3.4 litres	6 pints
3.9 litres	7 pints
5 litres	8 pints (1 gal)

Oven temperatures

140°C	275°F	Gas Mk 1
150°C	300°F	Gas Mk 2
160°C	325°F	Gas Mk 3
180°C	350°F	Gas Mk 4
190°C	375°F	Gas Mk 5
200°C	400°F	Gas Mk 6
220°C	425°F	Gas Mk 7
230°C	450°F	Gas Mk 8
240°C	475°F	Gas Mk 9

*Conversions are approximate and have been rounded up or down.

Further Reading

Books

Intuitive Eating, 4th Edition: A Revolutionary Anti-Diet Approach, Evelyn Tribole and Elyse Resch

The Gentle Eating Book: The Easier, Calmer Approach to Feeding Your Child and Solving Common Eating Problems, Sarah Ockwell Smith

Body Happy Kids: How to help children and teens love the skin they're in, Molly Forbes

First Bite: How We Learn to Eat, Bee Wilson

Born To Eat, Leslie Schilling and Wendy Jo Peterson

Websites

NHS Start4Life Website
www.nhs.uk/start4life

The Ellyn Satter Institute
ellynsatterinstitute.org

Allergy UK
allergyuk.org

Red Cross Baby First Aid
www.redcross.org.uk/first-aid/learn-first-aid-for-babies-and-children

Index

Acknowledgements

I would firstly like to thank my husband for believing in Baby Led Kitchen and encouraging me to take great leaps of faith. I also thank him for being a pedant as they make the best recipe testers! Thank you to The Grandparents (A.K.A. our Covid support bubble). Your generous help meant I could steal pockets of time to write and cook. Thank you to my friend Katie McGhee, Senior Lecturer in Child Health Nursing at the University of East Anglia, for introducing me to Intuitive Eating and for helping me to compile my evidence. Thank you to another friend, Anna (registered dietician) for keeping my nutritional understanding up to date. Thank you, Sam and Leah, and all of the team at Ebury Books for setting this amazing challenge – what an opportunity. Thank you to the gorgeous babies who feature in this book (and to their grown-ups, of course). Thank you to my Instagram followers for liking, sharing, commenting and supporting me – without you, this book would not have been possible.

Lastly, thank you to my three beautiful children. Thank you for waiting 'just one minute' while I finished typing sentences. Thank you for watching TV for a bit while I scribbled down recipes. Thank you for stirring the cake mix, mashing the potatoes, chopping the mushrooms and scooping the flour. Thank you for challenging me and inspiring me every single day.

1

Vermilion, an imprint of Ebury Publishing,
20 Vauxhall Bridge Road, London SW1V 2SA

Vermilion is part of the Penguin Random House group of companies whose addresses can be found at global. penguinrandomhouse.com

 Penguin Random House UK

Text © Jo Weston 2022
Photography (all except pages 2, 4–5) © Haarala Hamilton 2022
Photography (pages 2, 4–5) © Katherine Ashdown 2022
Textured background © Corri Seizinger, Adobe Stock
Pattern motifs © viktoriayams, Adobe Stock
Design & illustrations © maru studio 2022

Jo Weston has asserted her right to be identified as the author of this Work in accordance with the Copyright, Designs and Patents Act 1988

First published by Vermilion in 2022
www.penguin.co.uk

A CIP catalogue record for this book is available from the British Library

Commissioning Editor: Sam Jackson
Project Editor: Leah Feltham
Editor: Kate Reeves-Brown
Designer & Illustrator: maru studio
Photographer: Haarala Hamilton
Author & family photographs: Katherine Ashdown
Food Stylist: Katy McClelland
Prop Stylist: Hannah Wilkinson

ISBN 9781785043888

Printed and bound in China by C&C Offset Printing Co., Ltd

The authorised representative in the EEA is Penguin Random House Ireland, Morrison Chambers, 32 Nassau Street, Dublin D02 YH68

 MIX
Paper from responsible sources
FSC® C018179

Penguin Random House is committed to a sustainable future for our business, our readers and our planet. This book is made from Forest Stewardship Council® certified paper.